THE ORIGINAL LASER SUPERHERO
Issues 1 through 4

Written by Rebecca Thompson, Ph.D.

Illustrations by Kerry G. Johnson

Spectra: *The Original Laser Superhero Compilation (Issues 1-4)*

Written by Rebecca Thompson, Ph.D.

Illustrations by Kerry G. Johnson

Illustrations by David Ellis, *pages 51-56*

Published by the
American Physical Society © 2013 – All Rights Reserved

American Physical Society
One Physics Ellipse - 4th Floor
College Park, MD 20740-3844
www.aps.org

ISBN 978-1-4675-8031-1

Printed in the U.S.A.

A note from the author

This volume contains the first four issues of the series, *Spectra: The Original Laser Superhero*. Spectra was originally conceived of to promote LaserFest 2010, a celebration of the 50th anniversary of the first working laser. When she was first created as part of the PhysicsQuest program, none of us knew how popular Spectra would become. Over the years, we have seen five comics in the series, four trips to Comic Con International, over a million readers and at least a few celebrities interested in her adventures. We hope this is the first of many compilation editions.

To kids *(don't tell your parents):* If this is the first time you are reading the Spectra series, I really hope you enjoy it. A lot of it is based on my actual experiences in middle school, only I was way more awkward, had braces and was not a very good athlete. It's pretty great to get to rewrite my life the way I wished it would have been and not the way it was. It's also fun to pretend I had super powers.

I'm a physicist by training, which means I get to explore the world around me, and do things like look at why flowers buckle and what would happen if we had more than three dimensions. It's a great career and I hope it is one you might consider. If not, that's okay too. Just make sure you like what you're doing. But, even if you don't go on to do physics or science, I hope you will learn some anyway.

In fact, I hope you learn some science in these comics. All the science, right down to Spectra's powers, is real. That means, you can go to school and tell your teachers what you are learning here and they will be super impressed. Heck, you could even read these comics in class and not get in (too much) trouble.

To parents *(don't tell the kids):* Spectra originally began as a way to introduce middle school students to lasers and how they work. Most educational materials are written by people who vaguely remember what it was like to be in middle school and then create things based on that.

This creates dated material that doesn't accomplish the goals of drawing kids in and then teaching them; instead, the style is a neon sign saying *"I was written by an adult that wants you to learn something and look I'm making it fun! "* and nothing will turn kids off faster.

I also only vaguely remember what it was like to be in middle school, so unless I do research, I'm always in danger of creating the same old stale stuff. After countless hours of watching Nickelodeon and Disney Channel, I remembered the struggles of middle school, fitting in, independence, fights with friends, and the often questionable sense of humor and tried to write stories based on those. Add in some superheroes and physics and that's the Spectra series.

I hope you as parents find this cheesy, slightly cliche, too colorful and lacking any sort of sophisticated humor. If that's true, then your kid's will love it!

~ Rebecca Thompson

A note from the illustrator

It's been my pleasure to illustrate *Spectra: The Original Laser Superhero* comic book series as part of my job duties as Art Director for the American Physical Society.

I was excited when approached with the idea of creating an original and youthful superhero to celebrate the 50th anniversary of the laser. I had previously illustrated children's books, newspaper graphics, caricatures, greeting cards and other projects. Plus, I had already drawn graphics and illustrations for the PhysicsCentral's PhysicsQuest program. But working with Dr. Rebecca Thompson afforded me the opportunity to take the program into a different direction and gain a larger audience for the important project.

Since 2010, Spectra, her friends and all the villains have entertained millions of readers within the pages of the comic books and across social media. Additionally, having the opportunity to attend Comic Con International in San Diego shows the world that there's still room for independent and educational publishers to make a mark in the comic industry.

The science-based storylines of the Spectra series are entertaining, fun and a great educational tool for the next generation of students (and artists) interested in science, technology, engineering and mathematics (STEM).

Keep reading and enjoying the adventures of Spectra!

~ *Kerry G. Johnson*

THE ORIGINAL LASER SUPERHERO
Issues 1 through 4

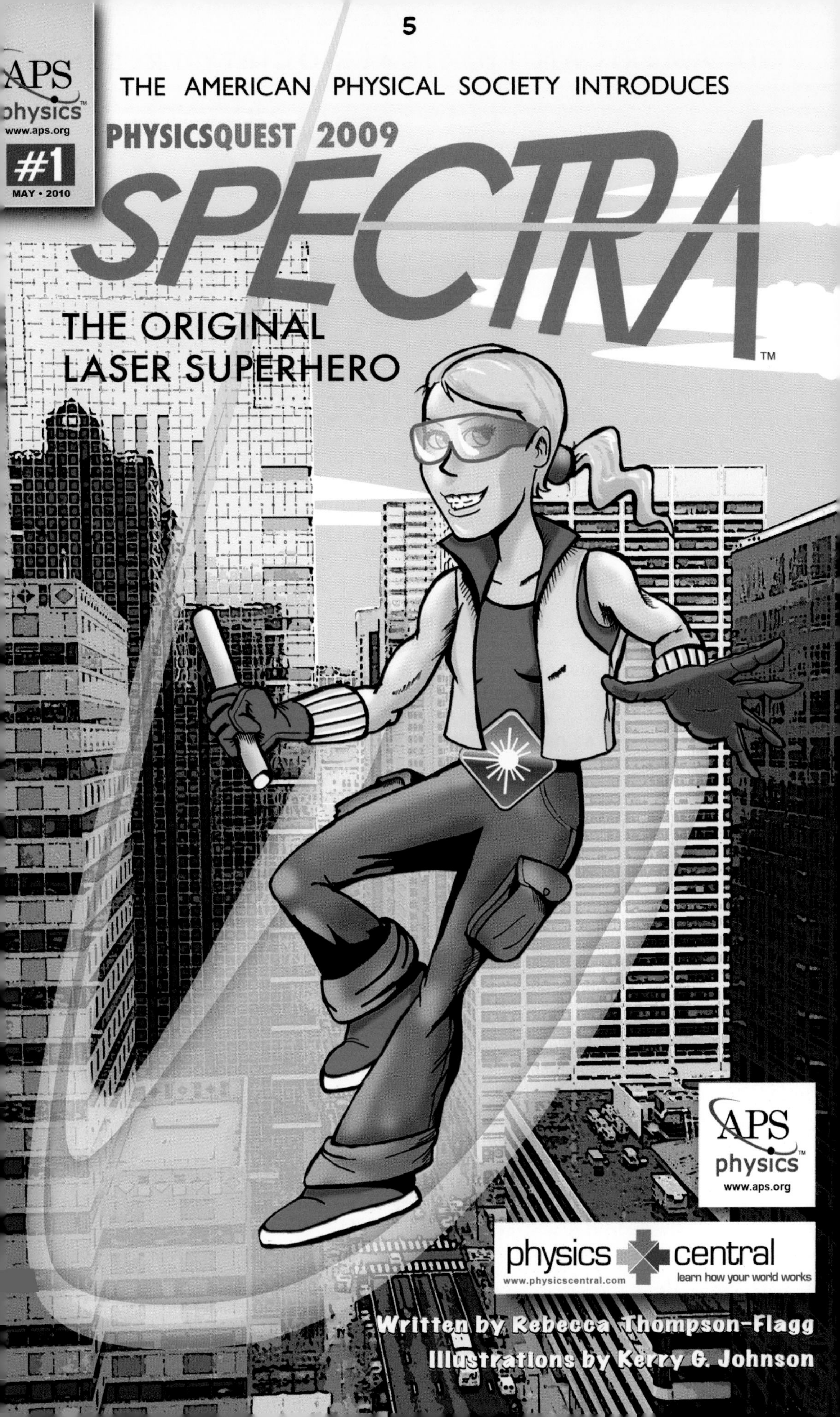
APS physics™
www.aps.org
#1
MAY • 2010
THE AMERICAN PHYSICAL SOCIETY INTRODUCES
PHYSICSQUEST 2009
SPECTRA™
THE ORIGINAL LASER SUPERHERO
APS physics™
www.aps.org
physics central
www.physicscentral.com
learn how your world works
Written by Rebecca Thompson-Flagg
Illustrations by Kerry G. Johnson

THE AMERICAN PHYSICAL SOCIETY PRESENTS

ABOUT THIS COMIC

The purpose of this comic is to teach both about the properties and history of one of the 20th century's most important inventions, the laser.

We have tried hard to make this comic fun and engaging while still being a great educational tool.

We would like to highlight the fact that the main character's names have been chosen with great care. For example, Lucinda's last name, Hene, is a reference to one of the most used types of lasers, a Helium Neon, or HeNe, laser.

Ruby was so named because the first laser was made with a synthetic ruby.

Gordy was named after Gordon Gould, one of the most controversial figures in laser history.

Kas was named after Alfred Kastler, physicist and Nobel prize winner, who developed the technique of "optical pumping" which is key to lasers. As for our villain, as any laser scientist knows, the death of any laser is misalignment.

To learn about Spectra and her friends, visit www.laserfest.org or www.physicscentral.com to download our first comic, *Spectra: The Original Laser Superhero!*

physics **central**
www.physicscentral.com learn how your world works

Characters Created by Rebecca Thompson, Ph.D. and Kerry G. Johnson

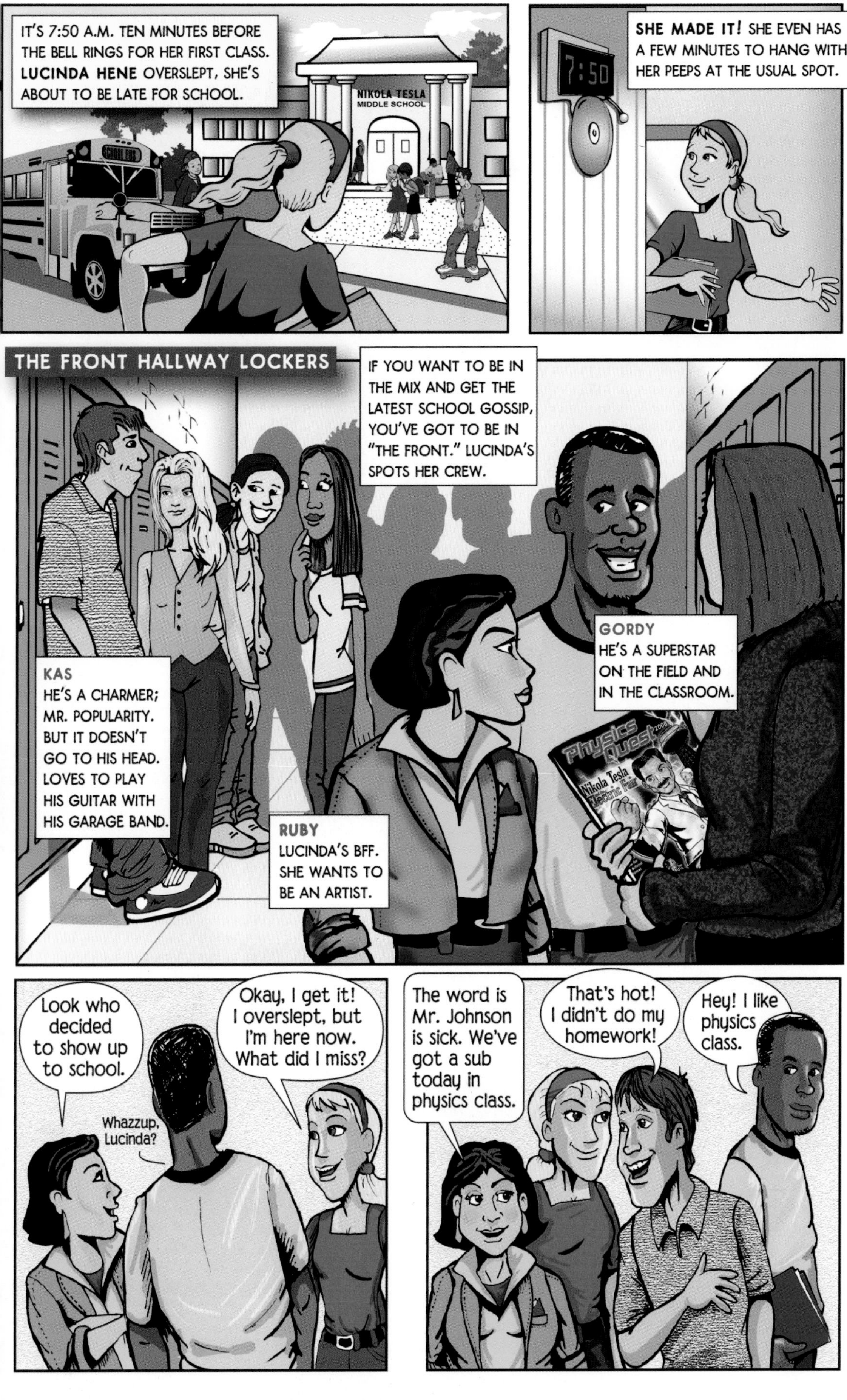
IT'S 7:50 A.M. TEN MINUTES BEFORE THE BELL RINGS FOR HER FIRST CLASS. LUCINDA HENE OVERSLEPT, SHE'S ABOUT TO BE LATE FOR SCHOOL.
NIKOLA TESLA MIDDLE SCHOOL
SCHOOL BUS
SHE MADE IT! SHE EVEN HAS A FEW MINUTES TO HANG WITH HER PEEPS AT THE USUAL SPOT.
7:50
THE FRONT HALLWAY LOCKERS
IF YOU WANT TO BE IN THE MIX AND GET THE LATEST SCHOOL GOSSIP, YOU'VE GOT TO BE IN "THE FRONT." LUCINDA'S SPOTS HER CREW.
KAS
HE'S A CHARMER; MR. POPULARITY. BUT IT DOESN'T GO TO HIS HEAD. LOVES TO PLAY HIS GUITAR WITH HIS GARAGE BAND.
RUBY
LUCINDA'S BFF. SHE WANTS TO BE AN ARTIST.
GORDY
HE'S A SUPERSTAR ON THE FIELD AND IN THE CLASSROOM.
Physics Quest 2008
Nikola Tesla Electric Fair
Look who decided to show up to school.
Whazzup, Lucinda?
Okay, I get it! I overslept, but I'm here now. What did I miss?
The word is Mr. Johnson is sick. We've got a sub today in physics class.
That's hot! I didn't do my homework!
Hey! I like physics class.

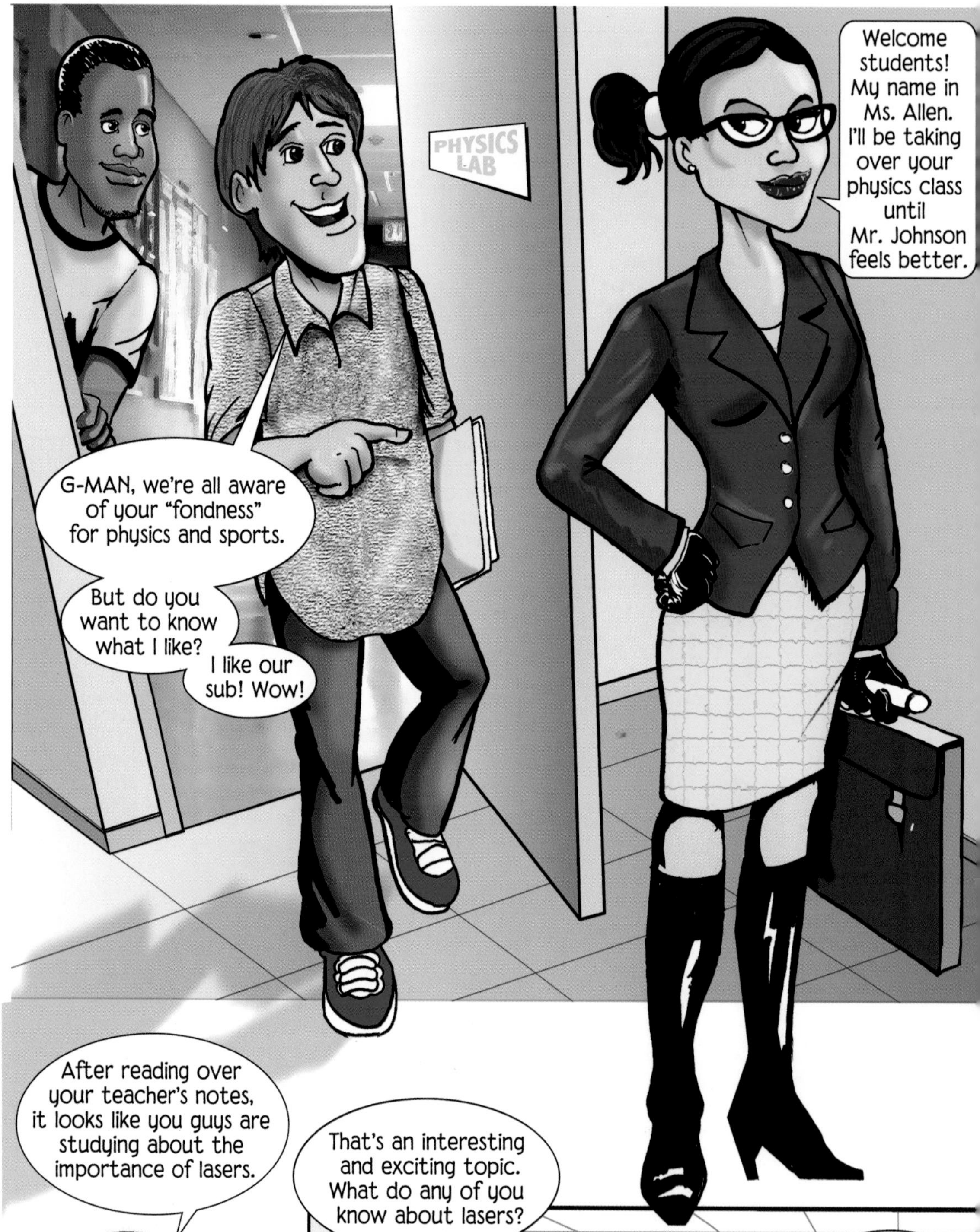
Welcome students! My name in Ms. Allen. I'll be taking over your physics class until Mr. Johnson feels better.
PHYSICS LAB
G-MAN, we're all aware of your "fondness" for physics and sports.
But do you want to know what I like?
I like our sub! Wow!

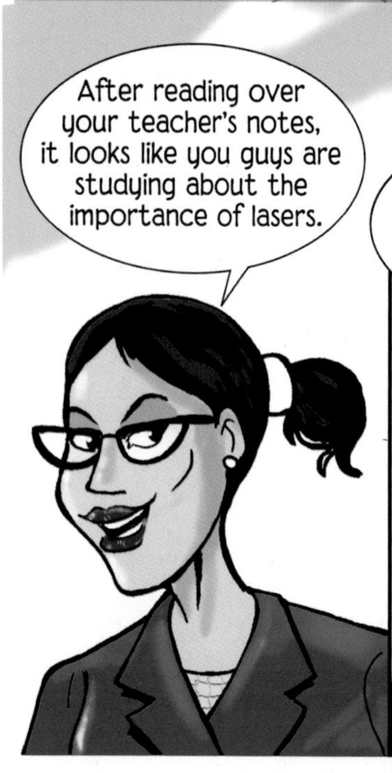
After reading over your teacher's notes, it looks like you guys are studying about the importance of lasers.

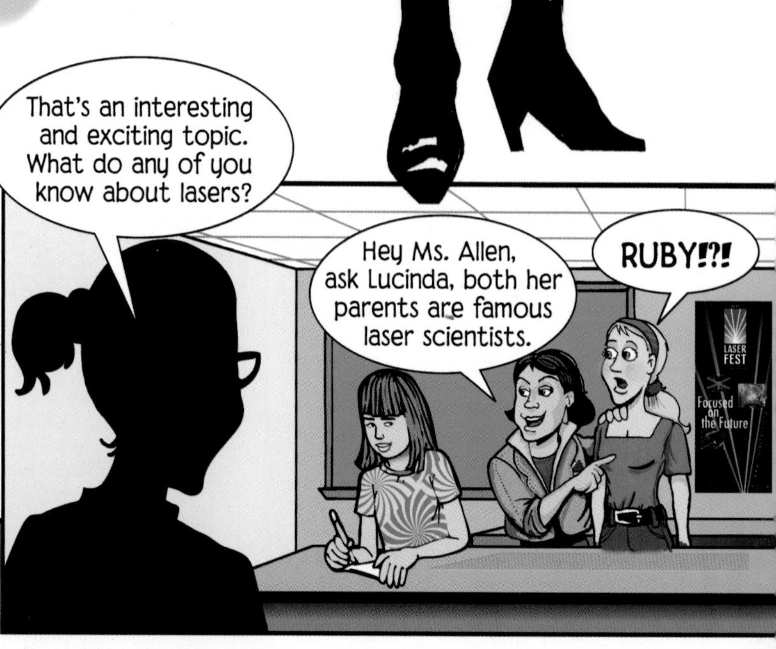
That's an interesting and exciting topic. What do any of you know about lasers?
Hey Ms. Allen, ask Lucinda, both her parents are famous laser scientists.
RUBY!?!
LASER FEST
Focused on the Future

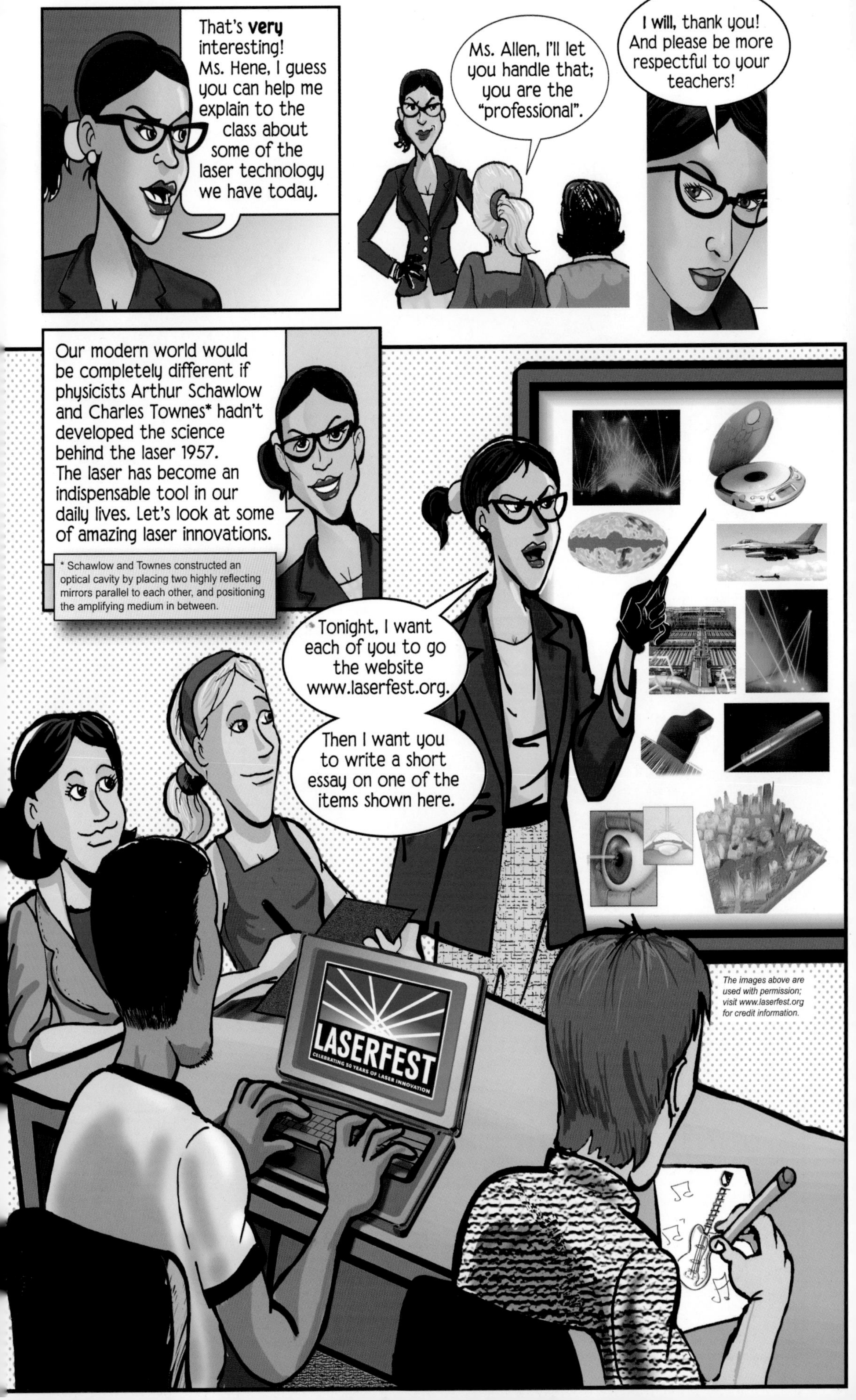

That's **very** interesting! Ms. Hene, I guess you can help me explain to the class about some of the laser technology we have today.
Ms. Allen, I'll let you handle that; you are the "professional".
I will, thank you! And please be more respectful to your teachers!
Our modern world would be completely different if physicists Arthur Schawlow and Charles Townes* hadn't developed the science behind the laser 1957. The laser has become an indispensable tool in our daily lives. Let's look at some of amazing laser innovations.
* Schawlow and Townes constructed an optical cavity by placing two highly reflecting mirrors parallel to each other, and positioning the amplifying medium in between.
Tonight, I want each of you to go the website www.laserfest.org.
Then I want you to write a short essay on one of the items shown here.
LASERFEST
CELEBRATING 50 YEARS OF LASER INNOVATION
The images above are used with permission; visit www.laserfest.org for credit information.

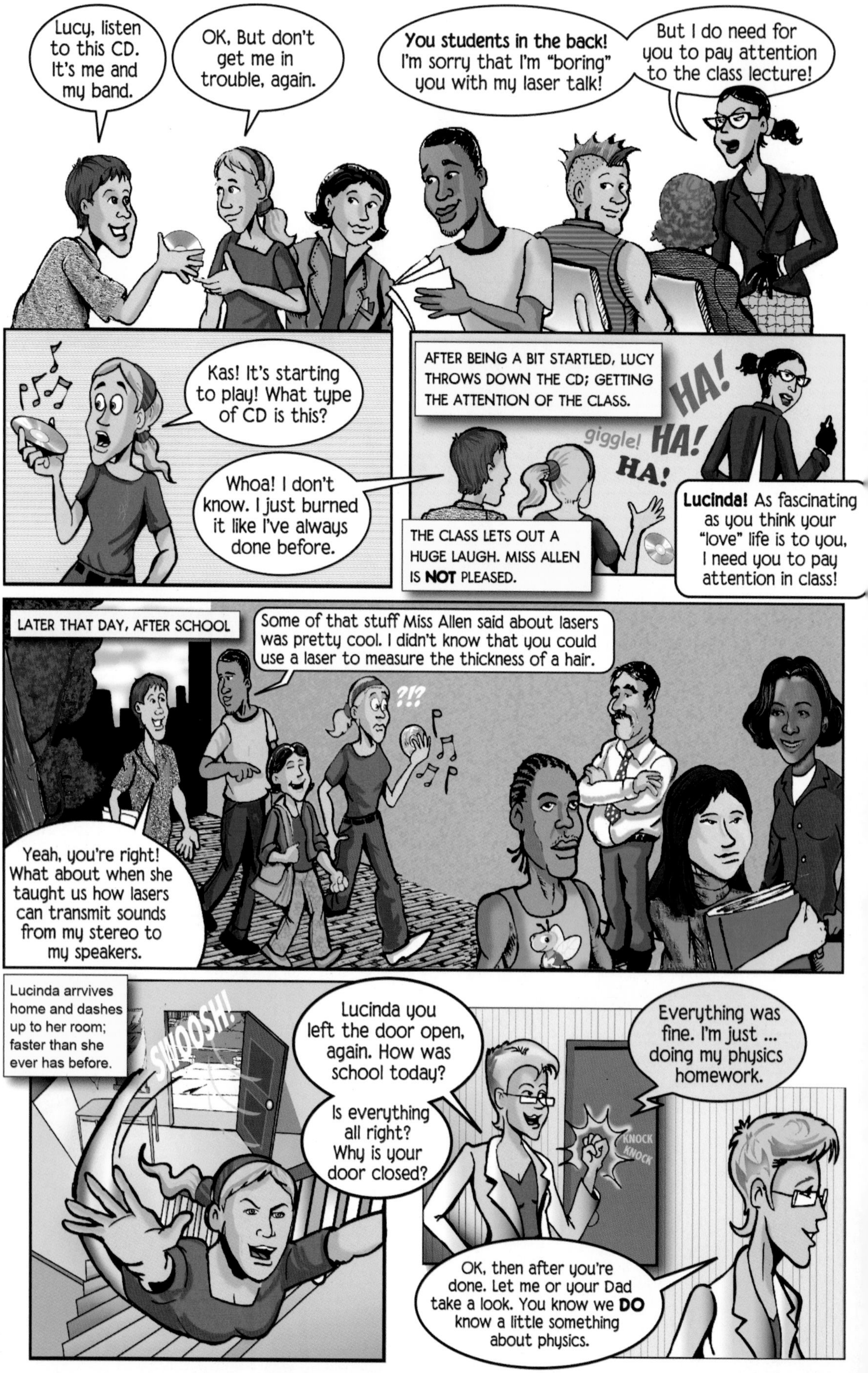
Lucy, listen to this CD. It's me and my band.
OK, But don't get me in trouble, again.
You students in the back! I'm sorry that I'm "boring" you with my laser talk!
But I do need for you to pay attention to the class lecture!
Kas! It's starting to play! What type of CD is this?
Whoa! I don't know. I just burned it like I've always done before.
AFTER BEING A BIT STARTLED, LUCY THROWS DOWN THE CD; GETTING THE ATTENTION OF THE CLASS.
HA! HA! HA!
giggle!
THE CLASS LETS OUT A HUGE LAUGH. MISS ALLEN IS NOT PLEASED.
Lucinda! As fascinating as you think your "love" life is to you, I need you to pay attention in class!
LATER THAT DAY, AFTER SCHOOL
Some of that stuff Miss Allen said about lasers was pretty cool. I didn't know that you could use a laser to measure the thickness of a hair.
?!?
Yeah, you're right! What about when she taught us how lasers can transmit sounds from my stereo to my speakers.
Lucinda arrvives home and dashes up to her room; faster than she ever has before.
SWOOSH!
Lucinda you left the door open, again. How was school today?
Is everything all right? Why is your door closed?
KNOCK KNOCK
Everything was fine. I'm just ... doing my physics homework.
OK, then after you're done. Let me or your Dad take a look. You know we DO know a little something about physics.

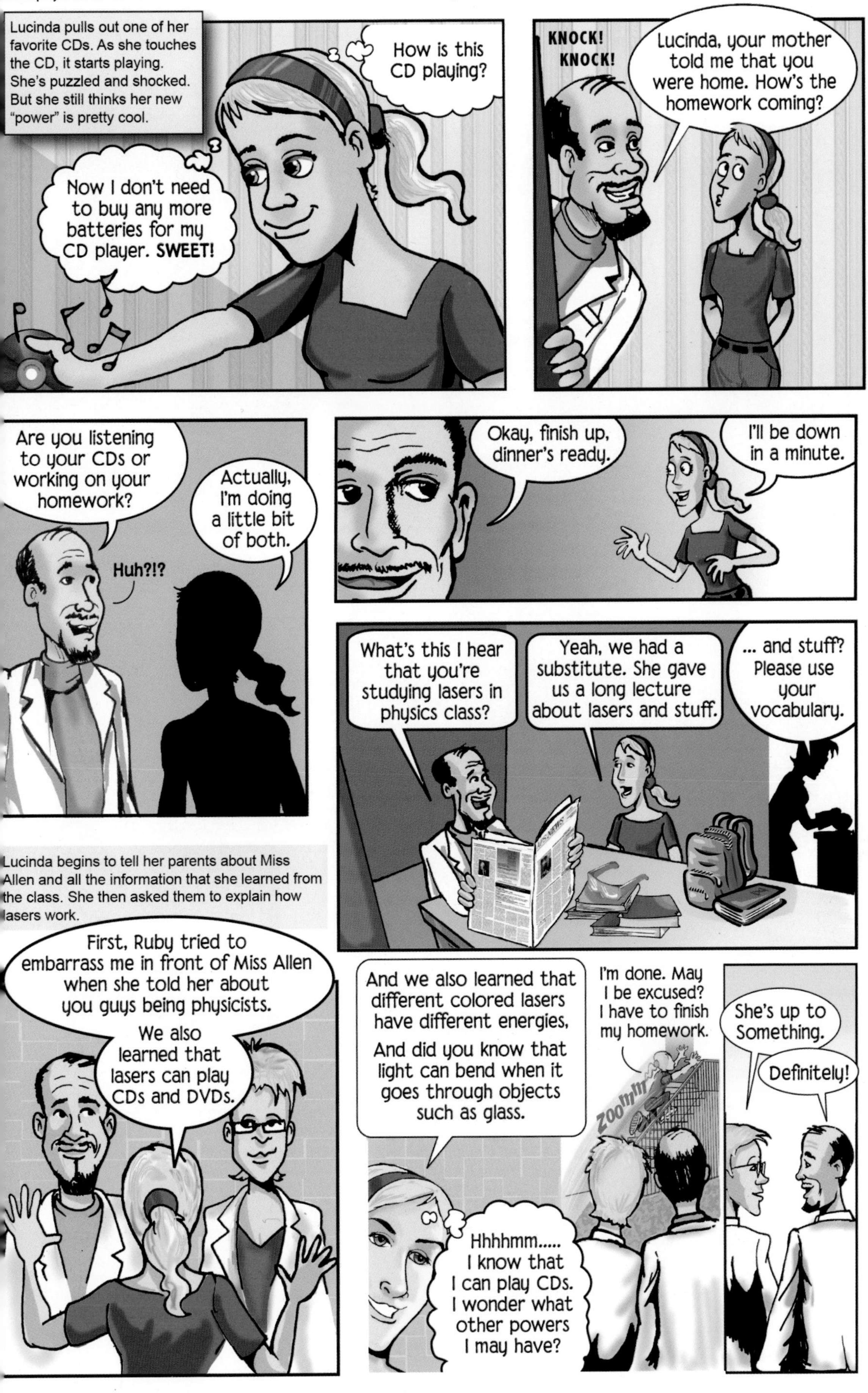
Lucinda pulls out one of her favorite CDs. As she touches the CD, it starts playing. She's puzzled and shocked. But she still thinks her new "power" is pretty cool.
How is this CD playing?
Now I don't need to buy any more batteries for my CD player. SWEET!
KNOCK! KNOCK!
Lucinda, your mother told me that you were home. How's the homework coming?
Are you listening to your CDs or working on your homework?
Huh?!?
Actually, I'm doing a little bit of both.
Okay, finish up, dinner's ready.
I'll be down in a minute.
What's this I hear that you're studying lasers in physics class?
Yeah, we had a substitute. She gave us a long lecture about lasers and stuff.
... and stuff? Please use your vocabulary.
Lucinda begins to tell her parents about Miss Allen and all the information that she learned from the class. She then asked them to explain how lasers work.
First, Ruby tried to embarrass me in front of Miss Allen when she told her about you guys being physicists.
We also learned that lasers can play CDs and DVDs.
And we also learned that different colored lasers have different energies,
And did you know that light can bend when it goes through objects such as glass.
Hhhhmm..... I know that I can play CDs. I wonder what other powers I may have?
I'm done. May I be excused? I have to finish my homework.
Zoom
She's up to Something.
Definitely!

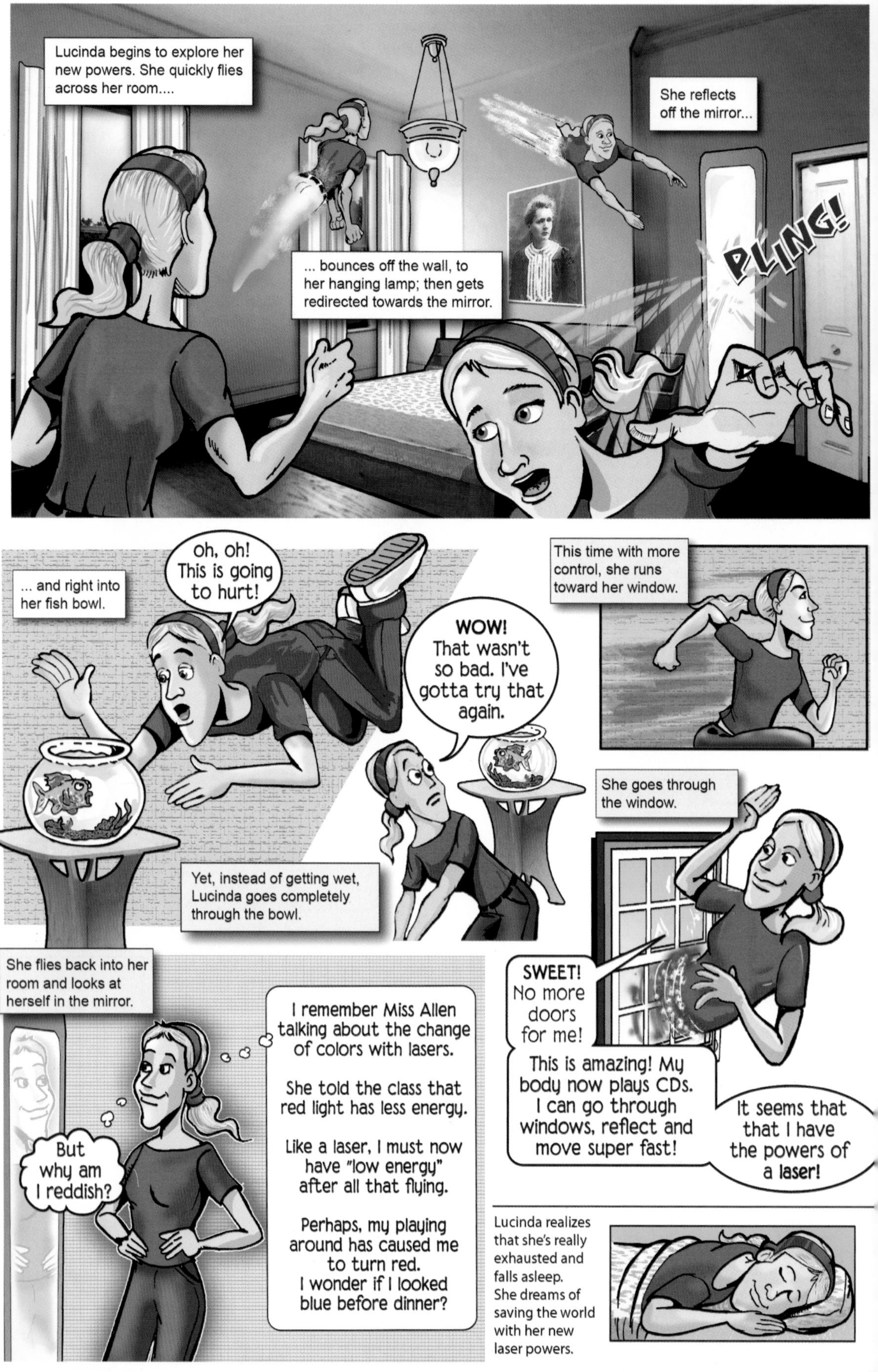
Lucinda begins to explore her new powers. She quickly flies across her room....
... bounces off the wall, to her hanging lamp; then gets redirected towards the mirror.
She reflects off the mirror...
PLING!
... and right into her fish bowl.
Oh, oh! This is going to hurt!
Yet, instead of getting wet, Lucinda goes completely through the bowl.
WOW! That wasn't so bad. I've gotta try that again.
This time with more control, she runs toward her window.
She goes through the window.
SWEET! No more doors for me!
This is amazing! My body now plays CDs. I can go through windows, reflect and move super fast!
It seems that that I have the powers of a laser!
She flies back into her room and looks at herself in the mirror.
But why am I reddish?
I remember Miss Allen talking about the change of colors with lasers.
She told the class that red light has less energy.
Like a laser, I must now have "low energy" after all that flying.
Perhaps, my playing around has caused me to turn red.
I wonder if I looked blue before dinner?
Lucinda realizes that she's really exhausted and falls asleep. She dreams of saving the world with her new laser powers.

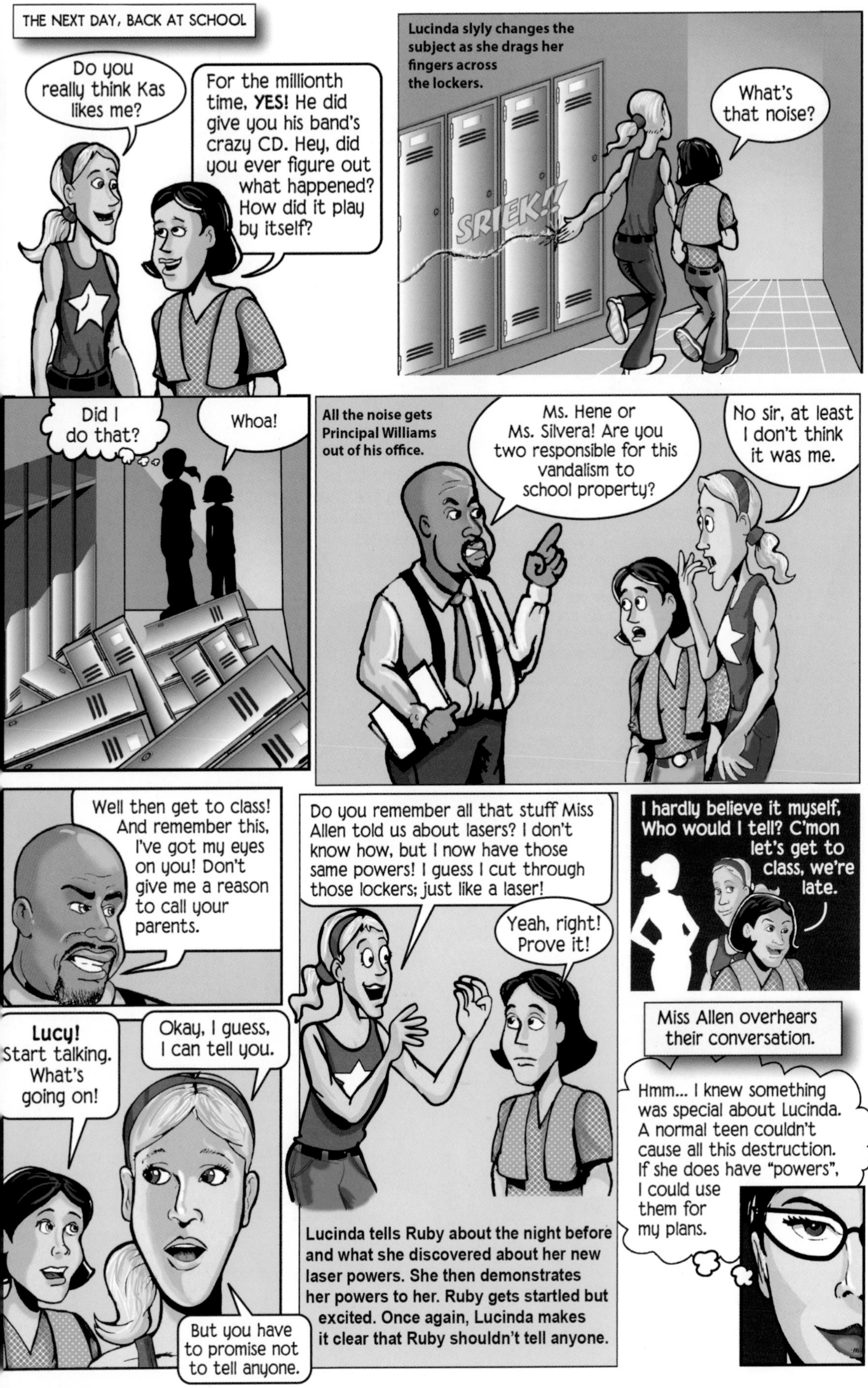
THE NEXT DAY, BACK AT SCHOOL
Do you really think Kas likes me?
For the millionth time, YES! He did give you his band's crazy CD. Hey, did you ever figure out what happened? How did it play by itself?
Lucinda slyly changes the subject as she drags her fingers across the lockers.
SRIEK!!
What's that noise?
Did I do that?
Whoa!
All the noise gets Principal Williams out of his office.
Ms. Hene or Ms. Silvera! Are you two responsible for this vandalism to school property?
No sir, at least I don't think it was me.
Well then get to class! And remember this, I've got my eyes on you! Don't give me a reason to call your parents.
Lucy! Start talking. What's going on!
Okay, I guess, I can tell you.
But you have to promise not to tell anyone.
Do you remember all that stuff Miss Allen told us about lasers? I don't know how, but I now have those same powers! I guess I cut through those lockers; just like a laser!
Yeah, right! Prove it!
Lucinda tells Ruby about the night before and what she discovered about her new laser powers. She then demonstrates her powers to her. Ruby gets startled but excited. Once again, Lucinda makes it clear that Ruby shouldn't tell anyone.
I hardly believe it myself, Who would I tell? C'mon let's get to class, we're late.
Miss Allen overhears their conversation.
Hmm... I knew something was special about Lucinda. A normal teen couldn't cause all this destruction. If she does have "powers", I could use them for my plans.

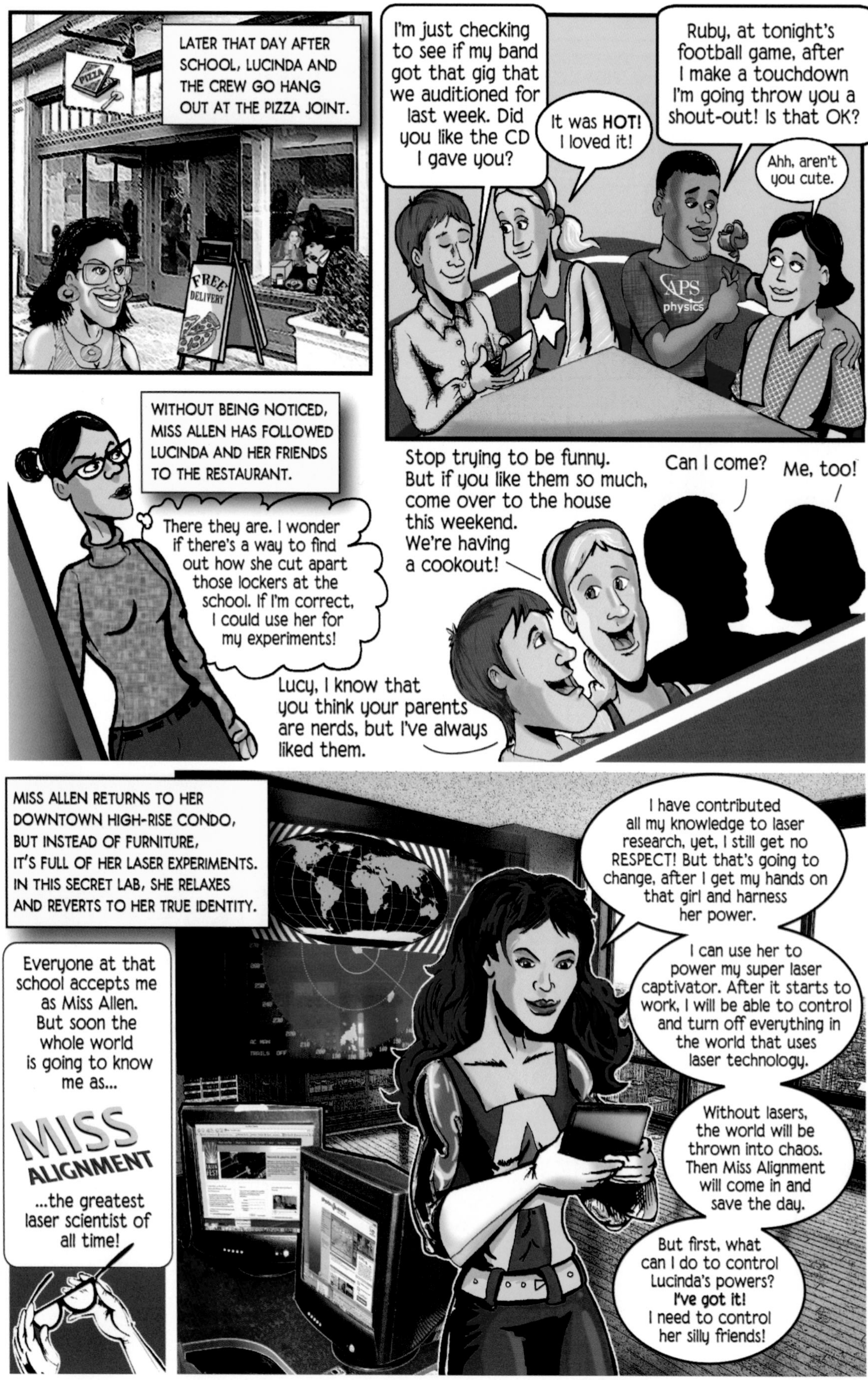
LATER THAT DAY AFTER SCHOOL, LUCINDA AND THE CREW GO HANG OUT AT THE PIZZA JOINT.
PIZZA
FREE DELIVERY
I'm just checking to see if my band got that gig that we auditioned for last week. Did you like the CD I gave you?
It was HOT! I loved it!
Ruby, at tonight's football game, after I make a touchdown I'm going throw you a shout-out! Is that OK?
Ahh, aren't you cute.
APS physics
WITHOUT BEING NOTICED, MISS ALLEN HAS FOLLOWED LUCINDA AND HER FRIENDS TO THE RESTAURANT.
There they are. I wonder if there's a way to find out how she cut apart those lockers at the school. If I'm correct, I could use her for my experiments!
Lucy, I know that you think your parents are nerds, but I've always liked them.
Stop trying to be funny. But if you like them so much, come over to the house this weekend. We're having a cookout!
Can I come?
Me, too!
MISS ALLEN RETURNS TO HER DOWNTOWN HIGH-RISE CONDO, BUT INSTEAD OF FURNITURE, IT'S FULL OF HER LASER EXPERIMENTS. IN THIS SECRET LAB, SHE RELAXES AND REVERTS TO HER TRUE IDENTITY.
Everyone at that school accepts me as Miss Allen. But soon the whole world is going to know me as...
MISS ALIGNMENT
...the greatest laser scientist of all time!
I have contributed all my knowledge to laser research, yet, I still get no RESPECT! But that's going to change, after I get my hands on that girl and harness her power.
I can use her to power my super laser captivator. After it starts to work, I will be able to control and turn off everything in the world that uses laser technology.
Without lasers, the world will be thrown into chaos. Then Miss Alignment will come in and save the day.
But first, what can I do to control Lucinda's powers? I've got it! I need to control her silly friends!

MISS ALIGNMENT AKA "MISS ALLEN" WORKS ON DEVELOPING HER RELATIONSHIPS WITH EACH OF LUCINDA'S BUDDIES AS A FRIEND AND MENTOR. THEY SLOWLY BEGIN TO TRUST HER.

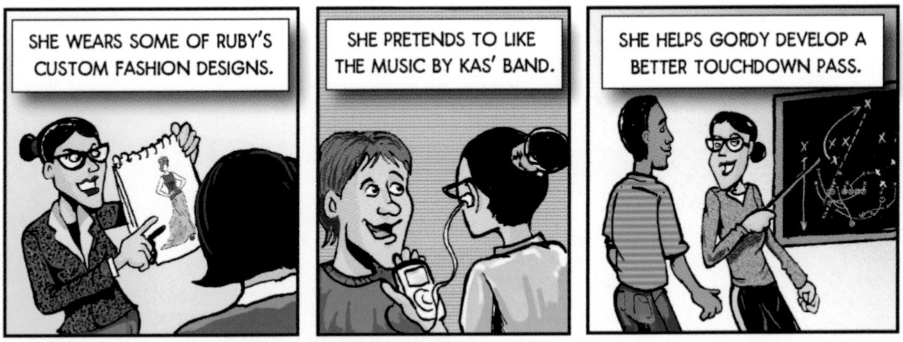
SHE WEARS SOME OF RUBY'S CUSTOM FASHION DESIGNS.
SHE PRETENDS TO LIKE THE MUSIC BY KAS' BAND.
SHE HELPS GORDY DEVELOP A BETTER TOUCHDOWN PASS.

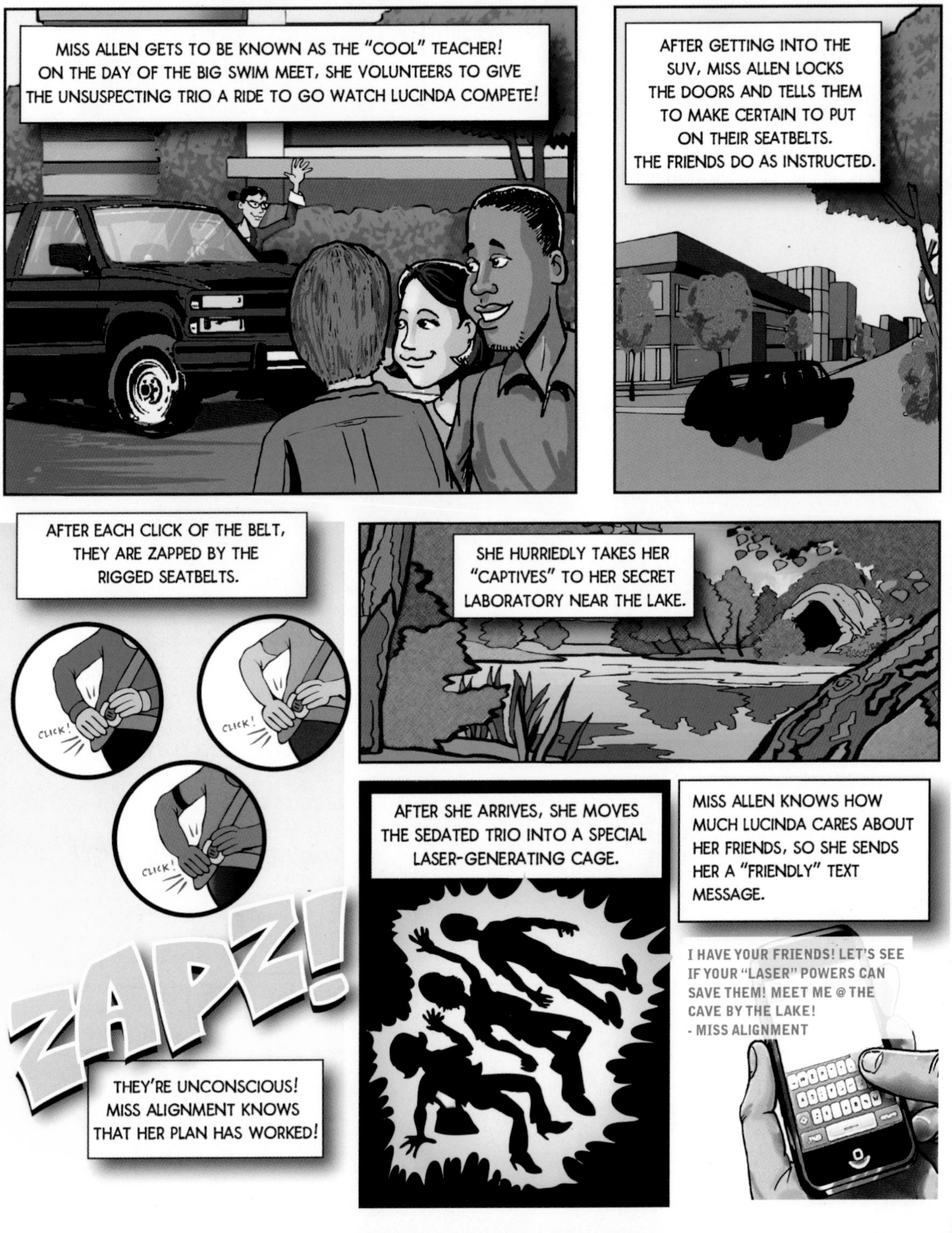
MISS ALLEN GETS TO BE KNOWN AS THE "COOL" TEACHER! ON THE DAY OF THE BIG SWIM MEET, SHE VOLUNTEERS TO GIVE THE UNSUSPECTING TRIO A RIDE TO GO WATCH LUCINDA COMPETE!
AFTER GETTING INTO THE SUV, MISS ALLEN LOCKS THE DOORS AND TELLS THEM TO MAKE CERTAIN TO PUT ON THEIR SEATBELTS. THE FRIENDS DO AS INSTRUCTED.
AFTER EACH CLICK OF THE BELT, THEY ARE ZAPPED BY THE RIGGED SEATBELTS.
CLICK!
CLICK!
CLICK!
ZAPZ!
THEY'RE UNCONSCIOUS! MISS ALIGNMENT KNOWS THAT HER PLAN HAS WORKED!
SHE HURRIEDLY TAKES HER "CAPTIVES" TO HER SECRET LABORATORY NEAR THE LAKE.
AFTER SHE ARRIVES, SHE MOVES THE SEDATED TRIO INTO A SPECIAL LASER-GENERATING CAGE.
MISS ALLEN KNOWS HOW MUCH LUCINDA CARES ABOUT HER FRIENDS, SO SHE SENDS HER A "FRIENDLY" TEXT MESSAGE.
I HAVE YOUR FRIENDS! LET'S SEE IF YOUR "LASER" POWERS CAN SAVE THEM! MEET ME @ THE CAVE BY THE LAKE!
- MISS ALIGNMENT

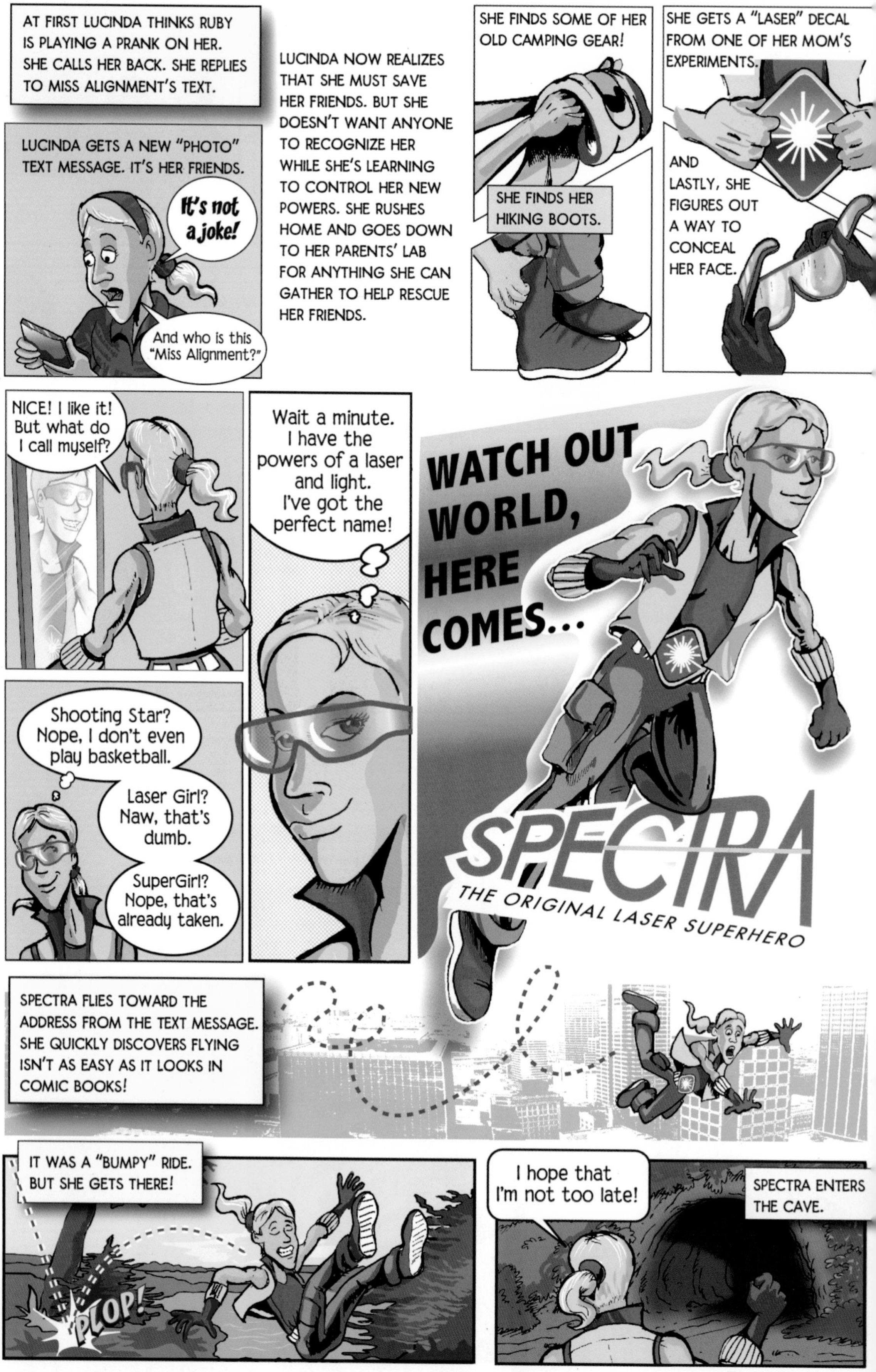
AT FIRST LUCINDA THINKS RUBY IS PLAYING A PRANK ON HER. SHE CALLS HER BACK. SHE REPLIES TO MISS ALIGNMENT'S TEXT.
LUCINDA GETS A NEW "PHOTO" TEXT MESSAGE. IT'S HER FRIENDS.
It's not a joke!
And who is this "Miss Alignment?"
LUCINDA NOW REALIZES THAT SHE MUST SAVE HER FRIENDS. BUT SHE DOESN'T WANT ANYONE TO RECOGNIZE HER WHILE SHE'S LEARNING TO CONTROL HER NEW POWERS. SHE RUSHES HOME AND GOES DOWN TO HER PARENTS' LAB FOR ANYTHING SHE CAN GATHER TO HELP RESCUE HER FRIENDS.
SHE FINDS SOME OF HER OLD CAMPING GEAR!
SHE FINDS HER HIKING BOOTS.
SHE GETS A "LASER" DECAL FROM ONE OF HER MOM'S EXPERIMENTS.
AND LASTLY, SHE FIGURES OUT A WAY TO CONCEAL HER FACE.
NICE! I like it! But what do I call myself?
Shooting Star? Nope, I don't even play basketball.
Laser Girl? Naw, that's dumb.
SuperGirl? Nope, that's already taken.
Wait a minute. I have the powers of a laser and light. I've got the perfect name!
WATCH OUT WORLD, HERE COMES...
SPECTRA
THE ORIGINAL LASER SUPERHERO
SPECTRA FLIES TOWARD THE ADDRESS FROM THE TEXT MESSAGE. SHE QUICKLY DISCOVERS FLYING ISN'T AS EASY AS IT LOOKS IN COMIC BOOKS!
IT WAS A "BUMPY" RIDE. BUT SHE GETS THERE!
PLOP!
I hope that I'm not too late!
SPECTRA ENTERS THE CAVE.

SPECTRA LOCATES HER FRIENDS INSIDE A LASER GENERATED CAGE.
I'm here to rescue you guys! Your friend Lucinda called me.
Thanks, but who are you?
I'm SPECTRA!
You're inspector; inspector of what?
NO! I said, Spectra!
Oh!
SPECTRA LOOKS AROUND AND SPOTS THE MAIN CONTROL SWITCH ON THE OTHER SIDE OF THE ROOM. BUT TO GET TO THE SWITCH, SHE MUST MANEUVER THROUGH THE DANGEROUS OBSTACLE COURSE SET UP BY MISS ALIGNMENT TO CHALLENGE SPECTRA'S LASER POWERS.
USING HER LASER POWERS, SPECTRA TACKLES EACH TASK,
She cuts through a solid metal door
She changes her wavelength color and appearance and blends into her surroundings
Hmm... it seems that I was right about Lucinda's powers or "Spectra" if that's what she's going by now!
She discovers a new power, "diffraction", which makes her split into several copies of herself.
She passes through a transparent window
After shutting down the lasers, Spectra rescues her friends.
Are you guys OK?
We're fine. But what about her?
Who?
Miss Allen is really Miss Alignment!
Not so fast little girl! Why do you think I kidnapped your friends and brought you here? I needed to see your POWER!
Miss Alignment quickly switches the cage's lasers back on!
I know that you think I'm small, but I have powers you can't believe!
Spectra tosses her goggles to Kas and yells to him to use them to deflect away Miss Alignment's lasers.
ZAPZZ
Wow! That worked!

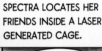

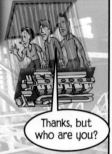

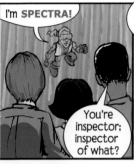

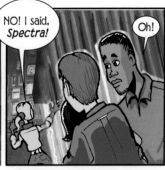

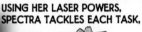

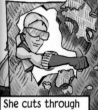

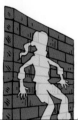

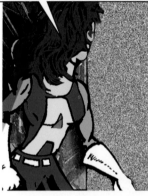

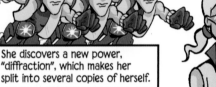

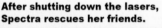

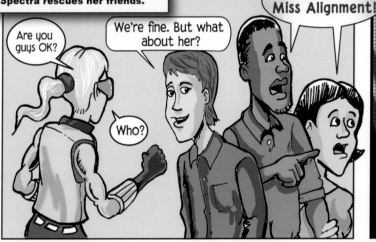

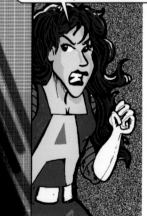

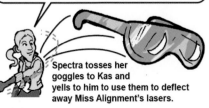

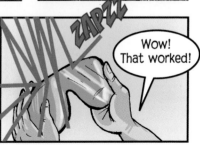

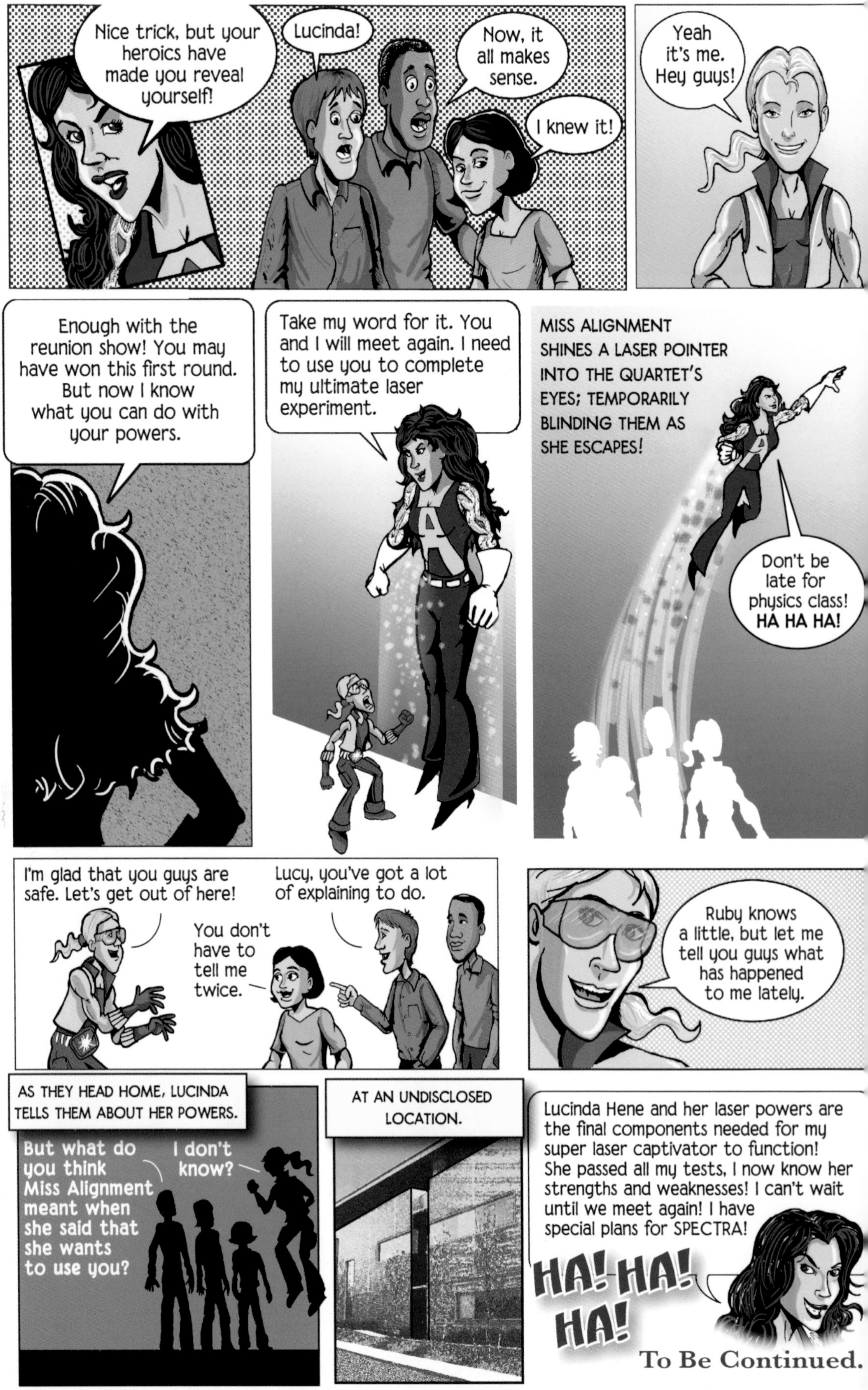
Nice trick, but your heroics have made you reveal yourself!
Lucinda!
Now, it all makes sense.
I knew it!
Yeah it's me. Hey guys!
Enough with the reunion show! You may have won this first round. But now I know what you can do with your powers.
Take my word for it. You and I will meet again. I need to use you to complete my ultimate laser experiment.
MISS ALIGNMENT SHINES A LASER POINTER INTO THE QUARTET'S EYES; TEMPORARILY BLINDING THEM AS SHE ESCAPES!
Don't be late for physics class! HA HA HA!
I'm glad that you guys are safe. Let's get out of here!
Lucy, you've got a lot of explaining to do.
You don't have to tell me twice.
Ruby knows a little, but let me tell you guys what has happened to me lately.
AS THEY HEAD HOME, LUCINDA TELLS THEM ABOUT HER POWERS.
But what do you think Miss Alignment meant when she said that she wants to use you?
I don't know?
AT AN UNDISCLOSED LOCATION.
Lucinda Hene and her laser powers are the final components needed for my super laser captivator to function! She passed all my tests, I now know her strengths and weaknesses! I can't wait until we meet again! I have special plans for SPECTRA!
HA! HA! HA!
To Be Continued.

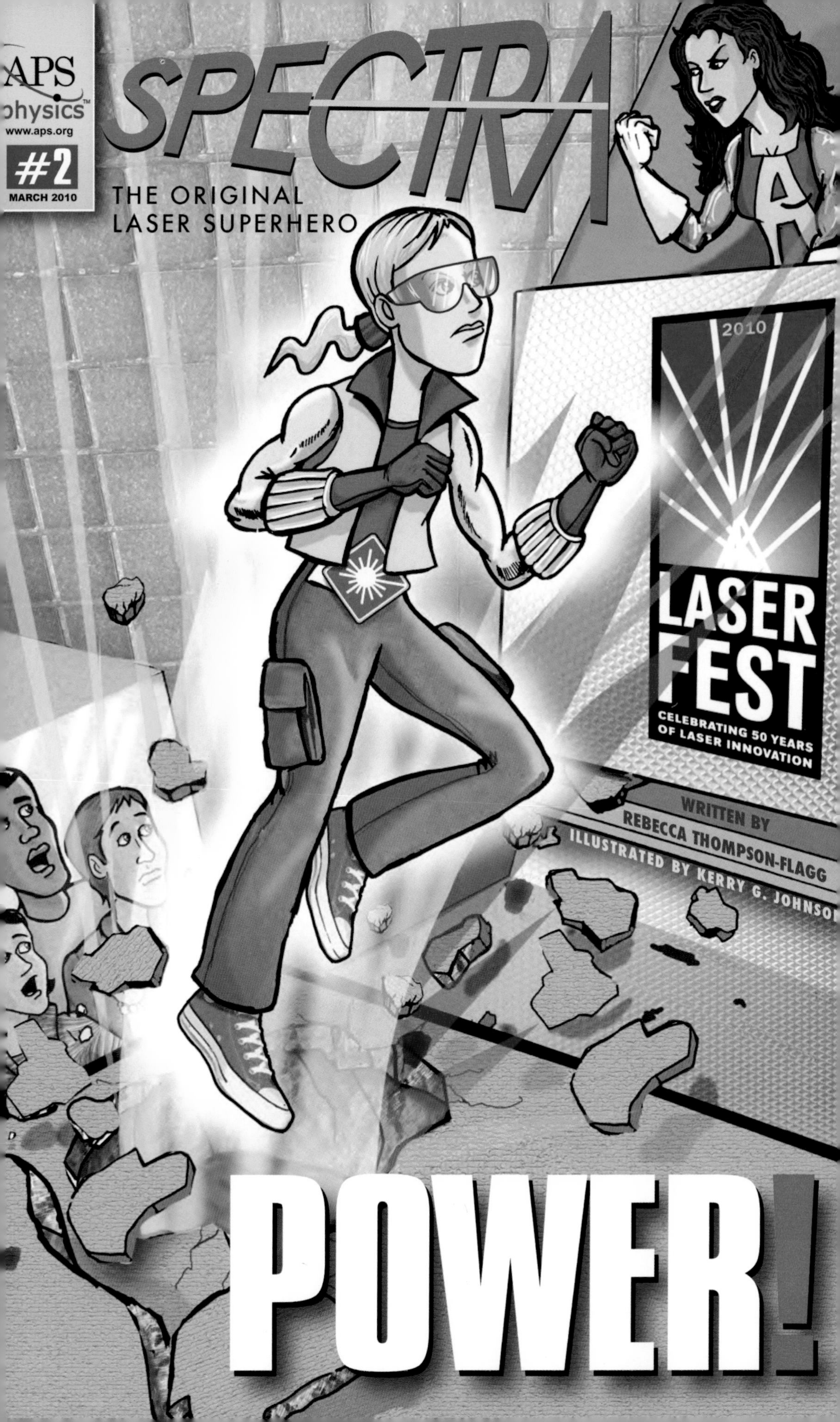
APS physics
www.aps.org
#2
MARCH 2010
SPECTRA
THE ORIGINAL LASER SUPERHERO
2010
LASER FEST
CELEBRATING 50 YEARS OF LASER INNOVATION
WRITTEN BY REBECCA THOMPSON-FLAGG
ILLUSTRATED BY KERRY G. JOHNSON
POWER!

SIX MONTHS HAVE PASSED SINCE LUCINDA HENE LEARNED ABOUT HER LASER POWERS. IN THE LAST ISSUE, SHE USED THOSE POWERS AS SPECTRA, TO RESCUE HER FRIENDS FROM THE CLUTCHES OF THE EVIL MISS ALIGNMENT. SINCE THAT "INCIDENT," THE GANG HAS HAD MANY OCCASIONS TO HAVE FUN WITH HER POWERS. BUT WHEN SHE'S NOT OUT SAVING THE WORLD, LUCINDA STILL HAS TO TAKE TIME TO STUDY FOR HER MIDTERM EXAMS WITH HER FRIENDS.

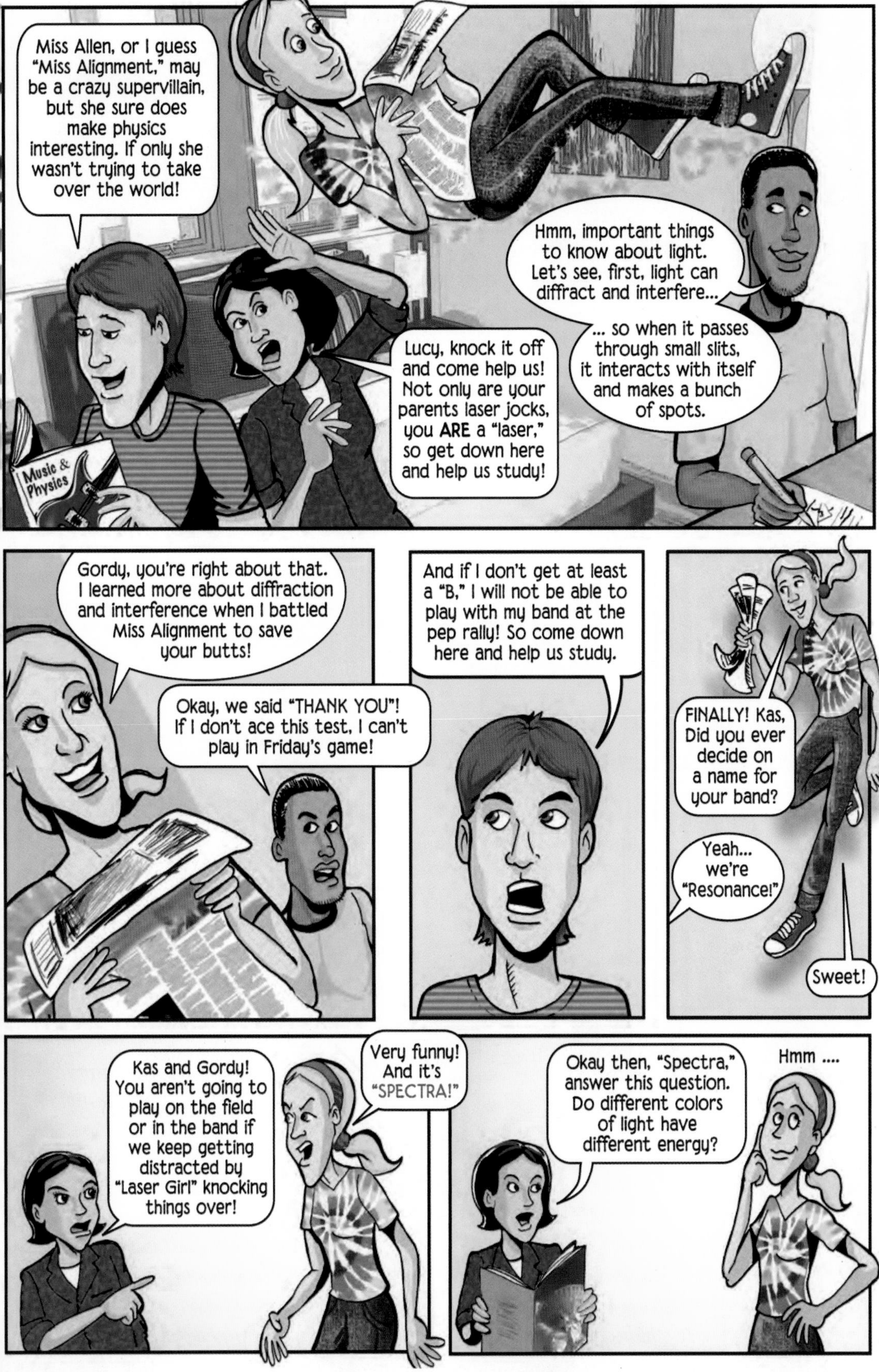
Miss Allen, or I guess "Miss Alignment," may be a crazy supervillain, but she sure does make physics interesting. If only she wasn't trying to take over the world!
Music & Physics
Lucy, knock it off and come help us! Not only are your parents laser jocks, you ARE a "laser," so get down here and help us study!
Hmm, important things to know about light. Let's see, first, light can diffract and interfere...
... so when it passes through small slits, it interacts with itself and makes a bunch of spots.
Gordy, you're right about that. I learned more about diffraction and interference when I battled Miss Alignment to save your butts!
Okay, we said "THANK YOU"! If I don't ace this test, I can't play in Friday's game!
And if I don't get at least a "B," I will not be able to play with my band at the pep rally! So come down here and help us study.
FINALLY! Kas, Did you ever decide on a name for your band?
Yeah... we're "Resonance!"
Sweet!
Kas and Gordy! You aren't going to play on the field or in the band if we keep getting distracted by "Laser Girl" knocking things over!
Very funny! And it's "SPECTRA!"
Okay then, "Spectra," answer this question. Do different colors of light have different energy?
Hmm ....

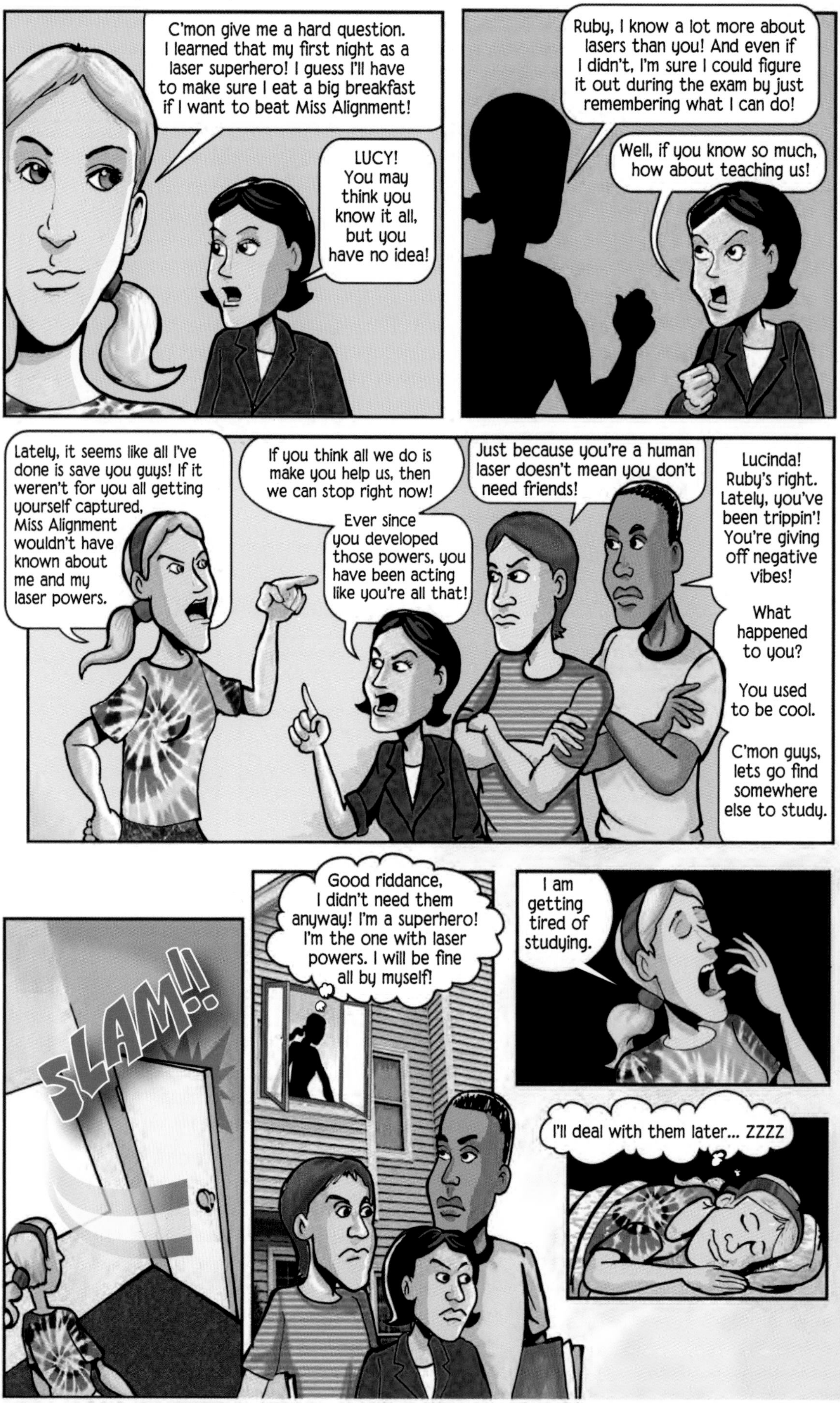
C'mon give me a hard question. I learned that my first night as a laser superhero! I guess I'll have to make sure I eat a big breakfast if I want to beat Miss Alignment!
LUCY! You may think you know it all, but you have no idea!
Ruby, I know a lot more about lasers than you! And even if I didn't, I'm sure I could figure it out during the exam by just remembering what I can do!
Well, if you know so much, how about teaching us!
Lately, it seems like all I've done is save you guys! If it weren't for you all getting yourself captured, Miss Alignment wouldn't have known about me and my laser powers.
If you think all we do is make you help us, then we can stop right now!
Ever since you developed those powers, you have been acting like you're all that!
Just because you're a human laser doesn't mean you don't need friends!
Lucinda! Ruby's right. Lately, you've been trippin'! You're giving off negative vibes!
What happened to you?
You used to be cool.
C'mon guys, lets go find somewhere else to study.
SLAM!!
Good riddance, I didn't need them anyway! I'm a superhero! I'm the one with laser powers. I will be fine all by myself!
I am getting tired of studying.
I'll deal with them later... ZZZZ

LATER THAT EVENING, A MYSTERIOUS FIGURE APPEARS ABOVE LUCINDA'S NEIGHBORHOOD.

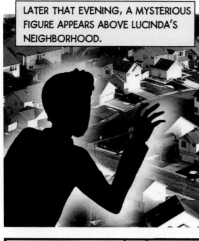

WHAT! Who are you? How did you get in my room?

Lucinda, I'm sorry that I startled you! I'm Irnee D'Haenens.*

I've read about you in my physics textbook. How is this possible? Am I dreaming?

Well... it's something like that.

*Irnee D'Haenens (1934 -2007) was a physicist who assisted Ted Maiman in making the first laser.

I have the powers of a laser so you better stand back!

Calm down. I already know that you're a living "laser"! I'm here to help and teach you about those special powers.

Whatcha talking about? I know how to use my powers! Do you want to try me! I actually know all about the laser!

Oh really? From the looks of the damage to this room, it's pretty obvious that you can't control your powers.

For example, do you know who invented the laser?

I read that a guy named Theodore Maiman demonstrated the first laser in 1960.

True, but do you really think he did it all by himself? Many people were involved in the creation of the laser, including me.

Change and put on your Spectra gear. Let's take a short trip back in history.

Okay, I'm ready! Where are we going?

You'll see. Just hold on!

Perhaps if you really understood the history behind the laser, you wouldn't waste your powerful gift on trivial things

SPECTRA AND IRNEE TRAVEL BACK IN TIME AND REAPPEAR IN THE LAB OF AMERICAN PHYSICIST THEODORE MAIMAN.

Don't worry, he can't see or hear us.

What just happened? Where are we?

We're back in 1960. This is Theodore Maiman's laboratory.

Is that you with Maiman? Were you there?

Yes, I was there and I saw the first laser light. Let's listen. Something special's about to happen.

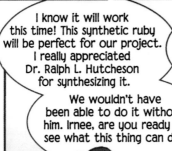

I know it will work this time! This synthetic ruby will be perfect for our project. I really appreciated Dr. Ralph L. Hutcheson for synthesizing it.

You bet! I may be color blind, but if this thing works, I'm sure even I will be able to see the red light.

We wouldn't have been able to do it without him. Irnee, are you ready to see what this thing can do?

Stand back! 3.. 2.. 1!

He didn't. He just made the first laser. But HOW to make the laser was someone else's idea. Actually, there's a lot of debate about whose idea it was. Let me explain.

BLIZZRT!!

And it was the first time that I saw the color red!

And it was made with a ruby. Just like my ex-BFF Ruby. But I'm doing fine without her.

Sure you are. I'm glad to hear it.

Here's another question for you. Where do you think the idea for the laser came from? Do you think Maiman came up with it all by himself?

Uhhmm.... I don't know.

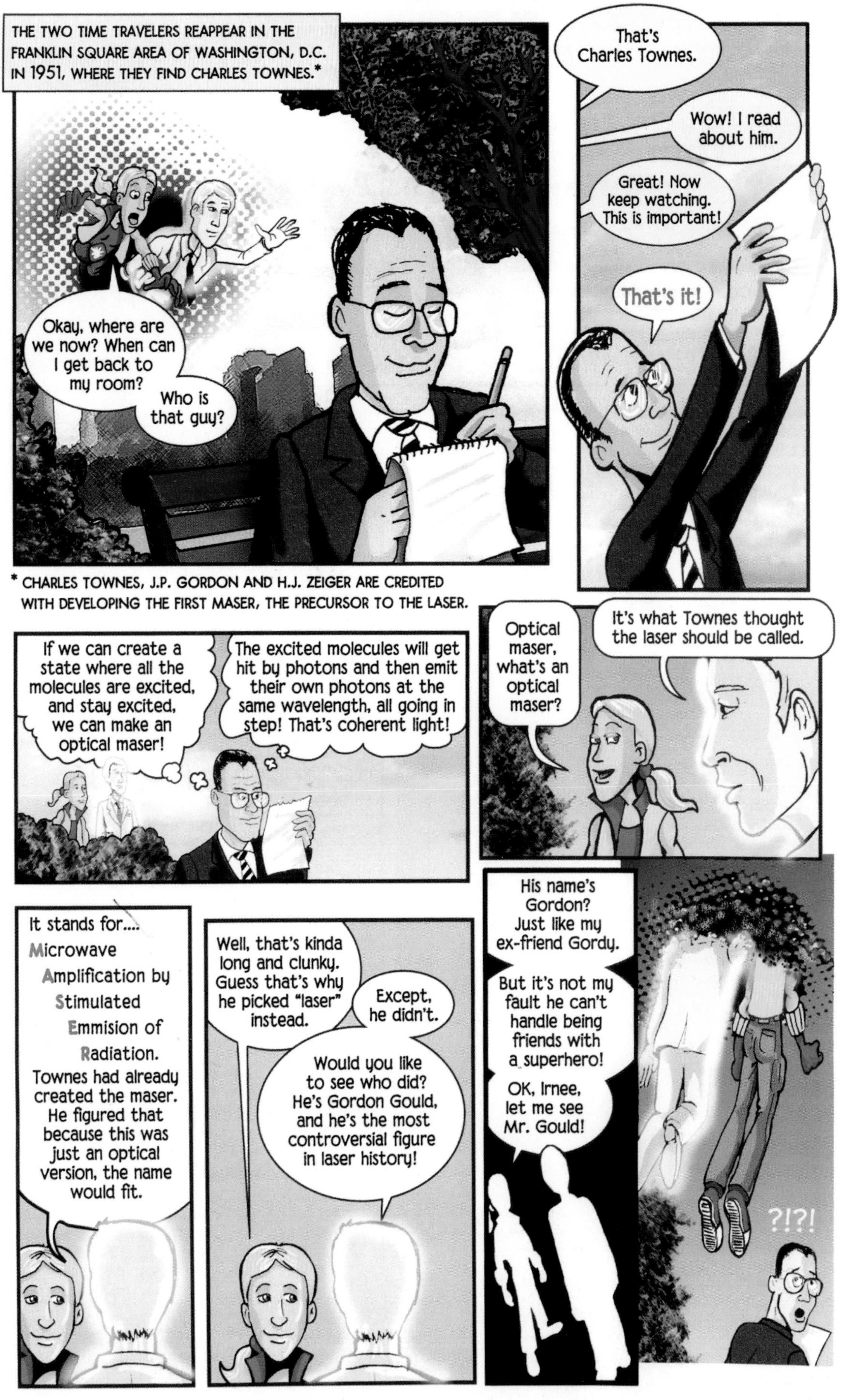
THE TWO TIME TRAVELERS REAPPEAR IN THE FRANKLIN SQUARE AREA OF WASHINGTON, D.C. IN 1951, WHERE THEY FIND CHARLES TOWNES.*
Okay, where are we now? When can I get back to my room?
Who is that guy?
That's Charles Townes.
Wow! I read about him.
Great! Now keep watching. This is important!
That's it!
* CHARLES TOWNES, J.P. GORDON AND H.J. ZEIGER ARE CREDITED WITH DEVELOPING THE FIRST MASER, THE PRECURSOR TO THE LASER.
If we can create a state where all the molecules are excited, and stay excited, we can make an optical maser!
The excited molecules will get hit by photons and then emit their own photons at the same wavelength, all going in step! That's coherent light!
Optical maser, what's an optical maser?
It's what Townes thought the laser should be called.
It stands for.... Microwave Amplification by Stimulated Emmision of Radiation. Townes had already created the maser. He figured that because this was just an optical version, the name would fit.
Well, that's kinda long and clunky. Guess that's why he picked "laser" instead.
Except, he didn't.
Would you like to see who did? He's Gordon Gould, and he's the most controversial figure in laser history!
His name's Gordon? Just like my ex-friend Gordy.
But it's not my fault he can't handle being friends with a superhero!
OK, Irnee, let me see Mr. Gould!
?!?!

SPECTRA AND IRNEE SOON ARRIVE AT THE HOME OF SCIENTIST, GORDON GOULD.

I have it!

* IN 1957, GORDON GOULD USED A DEVICE WITH MIRRORS THAT TRAPPED AND ISOLATED A SINGLE WAVELENGTH OF LIGHT. HE ALSO WAS THE FIRST PERSON TO USE THE TERM "LASER".

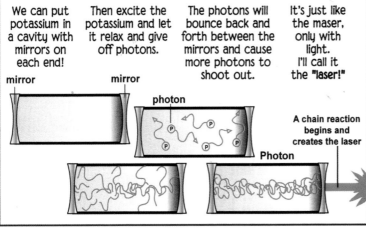

We can put potassium in a cavity with mirrors on each end!

Then excite the potassium and let it relax and give off photons.

The photons will bounce back and forth between the mirrors and cause more photons to shoot out.

It's just like the maser, only with light. I'll call it the "laser!"

mirror   mirror

photon

A chain reaction begins and creates the laser

Photon

Both Gordon Gould and Charles Townes say they were the original inventors of the laser.

They did work down the hall from each other. History has said that Townes did it first, but we don't call it the optical maser.

Are you beginning to see how many people were involved in the laser? No one person can do everything. You have to work together with colleagues and friends.

Well, maybe in science, but I can still save the world without my unappreciative former friends. In fact, I think Ruby, Gordy and Kas are jealous of my new super powers.

I'm sorry to hear that you still feel that way.

Whoa, look at the time. I have to get you back. You do have school.

SWEET! It's about time!

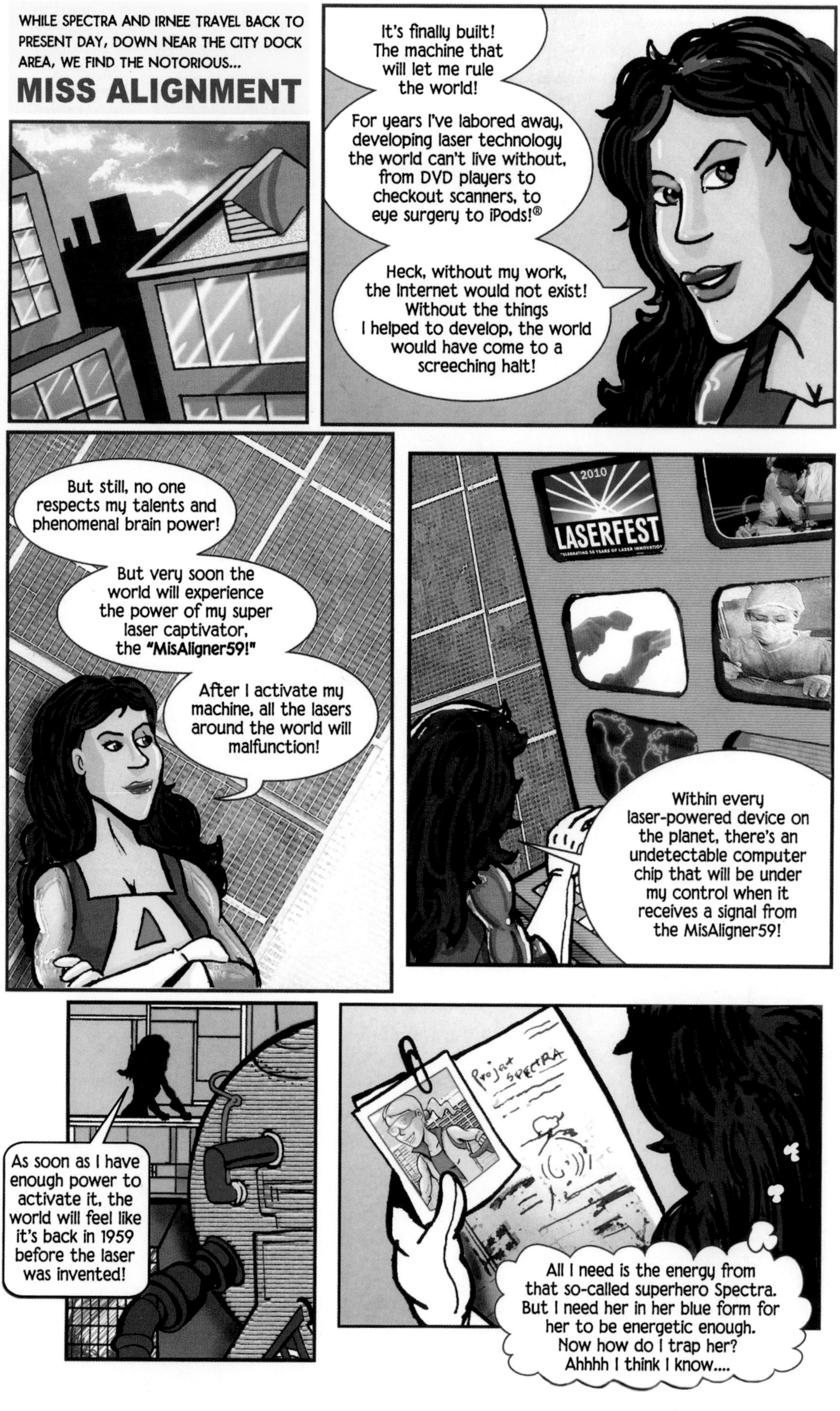
WHILE SPECTRA AND IRNEE TRAVEL BACK TO PRESENT DAY, DOWN NEAR THE CITY DOCK AREA, WE FIND THE NOTORIOUS...
MISS ALIGNMENT
It's finally built! The machine that will let me rule the world!
For years I've labored away, developing laser technology the world can't live without, from DVD players to checkout scanners, to eye surgery to iPods!®
Heck, without my work, the Internet would not exist! Without the things I helped to develop, the world would have come to a screeching halt!
But still, no one respects my talents and phenomenal brain power!
But very soon the world will experience the power of my super laser captivator, the "MisAligner59!"
After I activate my machine, all the lasers around the world will malfunction!
2010
LASERFEST
Within every laser-powered device on the planet, there's an undetectable computer chip that will be under my control when it receives a signal from the MisAligner59!
As soon as I have enough power to activate it, the world will feel like it's back in 1959 before the laser was invented!
Project SPECTRA
All I need is the energy from that so-called superhero Spectra. But I need her in her blue form for her to be energetic enough. Now how do I trap her? Ahhhh I think I know....

SPECTRA, *The Original Laser Superhero: #2 - March 2010*

PRESENT DAY

Wow, that was a weird dream!

Hhmm... but why am I in my costume?

The more that I think about yesterday, I was pretty rude to my "BFFs!" I REALLY do need them to be part of my life!

So one-by-one, Lucinda humbly calls Ruby, then Kas, and lastly Gordy to apologize. Everybody accepts. The crew's back together!

THE RECONNECTED FRIENDS LATER MEET UP AT THE PIZZA JOINT, WITHOUT KAS.

Lucy, did you ever figure out what Miss Alignment wanted from you?

Ruby, I've wondered about that. But I have no idea what she wants.

Don't worry about Miss A. You know if she tries anything, we've got your back!

I just got a text from Kas. He thought we were supposed to meet at the mall. He's there waiting for us. C'mon let's go.

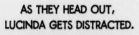

AS THEY HEAD OUT, LUCINDA GETS DISTRACTED.

Hey Lucy! WATCH OUT! You're about to walk into that pole!

Huh!?!

SLIIZZ!

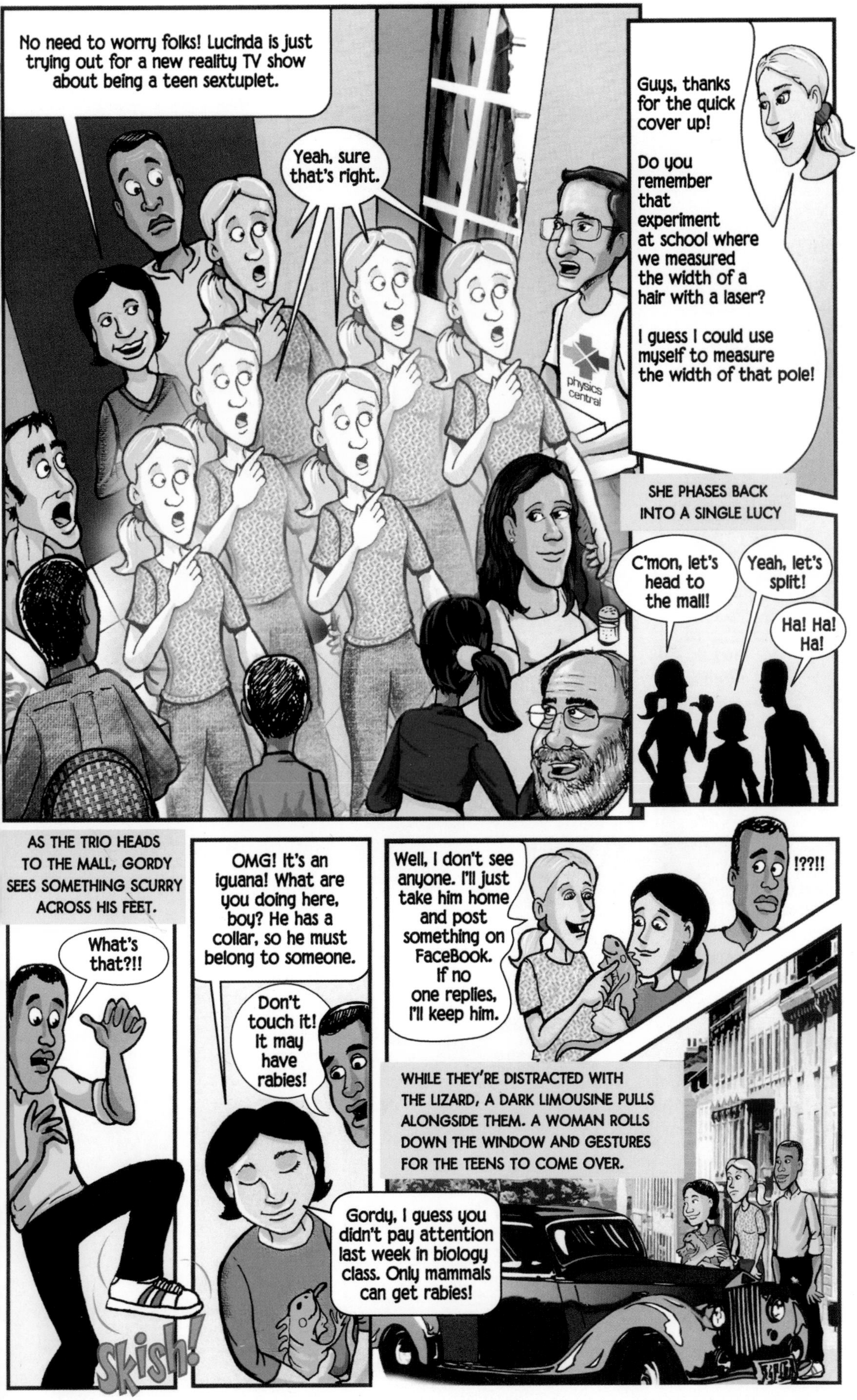
No need to worry folks! Lucinda is just trying out for a new reality TV show about being a teen sextuplet.
Yeah, sure that's right.
Guys, thanks for the quick cover up!
Do you remember that experiment at school where we measured the width of a hair with a laser?
I guess I could use myself to measure the width of that pole!
physics central
SHE PHASES BACK INTO A SINGLE LUCY
C'mon, let's head to the mall!
Yeah, let's split!
Ha! Ha! Ha!
AS THE TRIO HEADS TO THE MALL, GORDY SEES SOMETHING SCURRY ACROSS HIS FEET.
What's that?!!
Skish!
OMG! It's an iguana! What are you doing here, boy? He has a collar, so he must belong to someone.
Don't touch it! It may have rabies!
Gordy, I guess you didn't pay attention last week in biology class. Only mammals can get rabies!
Well, I don't see anyone. I'll just take him home and post something on FaceBook. If no one replies, I'll keep him.
!??!!
WHILE THEY'RE DISTRACTED WITH THE LIZARD, A DARK LIMOUSINE PULLS ALONGSIDE THEM. A WOMAN ROLLS DOWN THE WINDOW AND GESTURES FOR THE TEENS TO COME OVER.

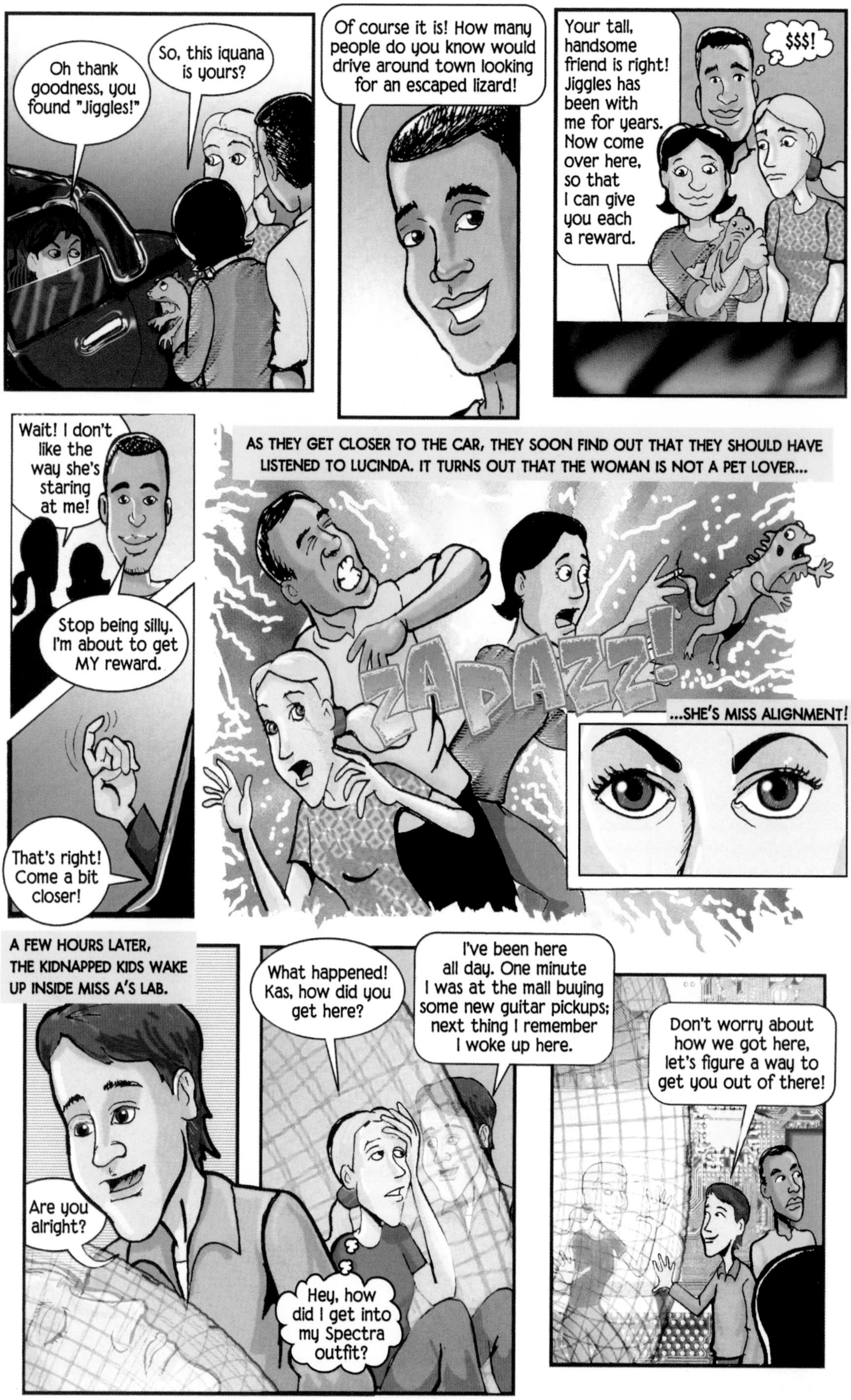
Oh thank goodness, you found "Jiggles!"
So, this iquana is yours?
Of course it is! How many people do you know would drive around town looking for an escaped lizard!
Your tall, handsome friend is right! Jiggles has been with me for years. Now come over here, so that I can give you each a reward.
$$$!
Wait! I don't like the way she's staring at me!
Stop being silly. I'm about to get MY reward.
That's right! Come a bit closer!
AS THEY GET CLOSER TO THE CAR, THEY SOON FIND OUT THAT THEY SHOULD HAVE LISTENED TO LUCINDA. IT TURNS OUT THAT THE WOMAN IS NOT A PET LOVER...
ZAPAZZ!
...SHE'S MISS ALIGNMENT!
A FEW HOURS LATER, THE KIDNAPPED KIDS WAKE UP INSIDE MISS A'S LAB.
Are you alright?
What happened! Kas, how did you get here?
I've been here all day. One minute I was at the mall buying some new guitar pickups; next thing I remember I woke up here.
Hey, how did I get into my Spectra outfit?
Don't worry about how we got here, let's figure a way to get you out of there!

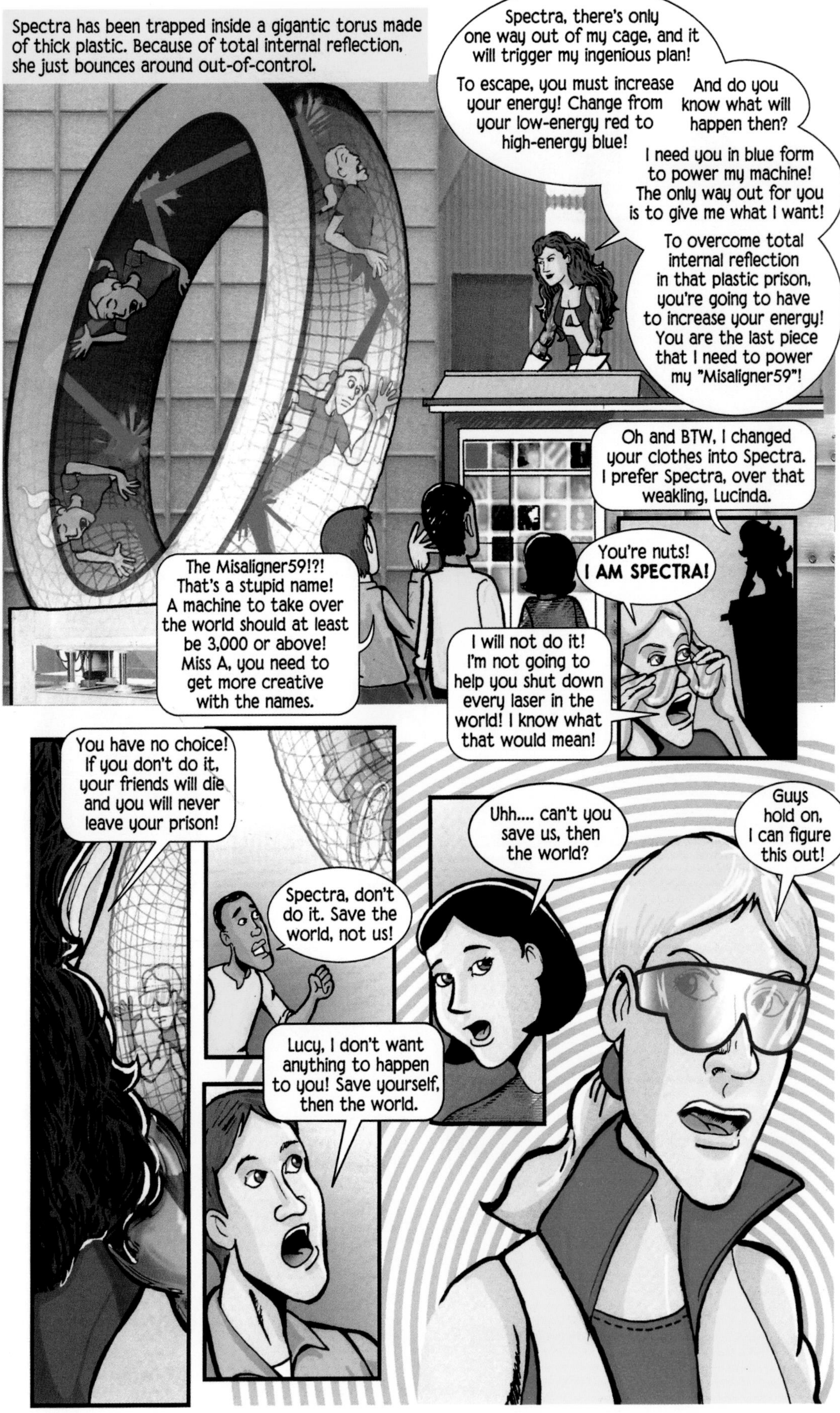
Spectra has been trapped inside a gigantic torus made of thick plastic. Because of total internal reflection, she just bounces around out-of-control.
Spectra, there's only one way out of my cage, and it will trigger my ingenious plan!
To escape, you must increase your energy! Change from your low-energy red to high-energy blue!
And do you know what will happen then?
I need you in blue form to power my machine! The only way out for you is to give me what I want!
To overcome total internal reflection in that plastic prison, you're going to have to increase your energy! You are the last piece that I need to power my "Misaligner59"!
The Misaligner59!?! That's a stupid name! A machine to take over the world should at least be 3,000 or above! Miss A, you need to get more creative with the names.
Oh and BTW, I changed your clothes into Spectra. I prefer Spectra, over that weakling, Lucinda.
You're nuts! I AM SPECTRA!
I will not do it! I'm not going to help you shut down every laser in the world! I know what that would mean!
You have no choice! If you don't do it, your friends will die and you will never leave your prison!
Spectra, don't do it. Save the world, not us!
Lucy, I don't want anything to happen to you! Save yourself, then the world.
Uhh.... can't you save us, then the world?
Guys hold on, I can figure this out!

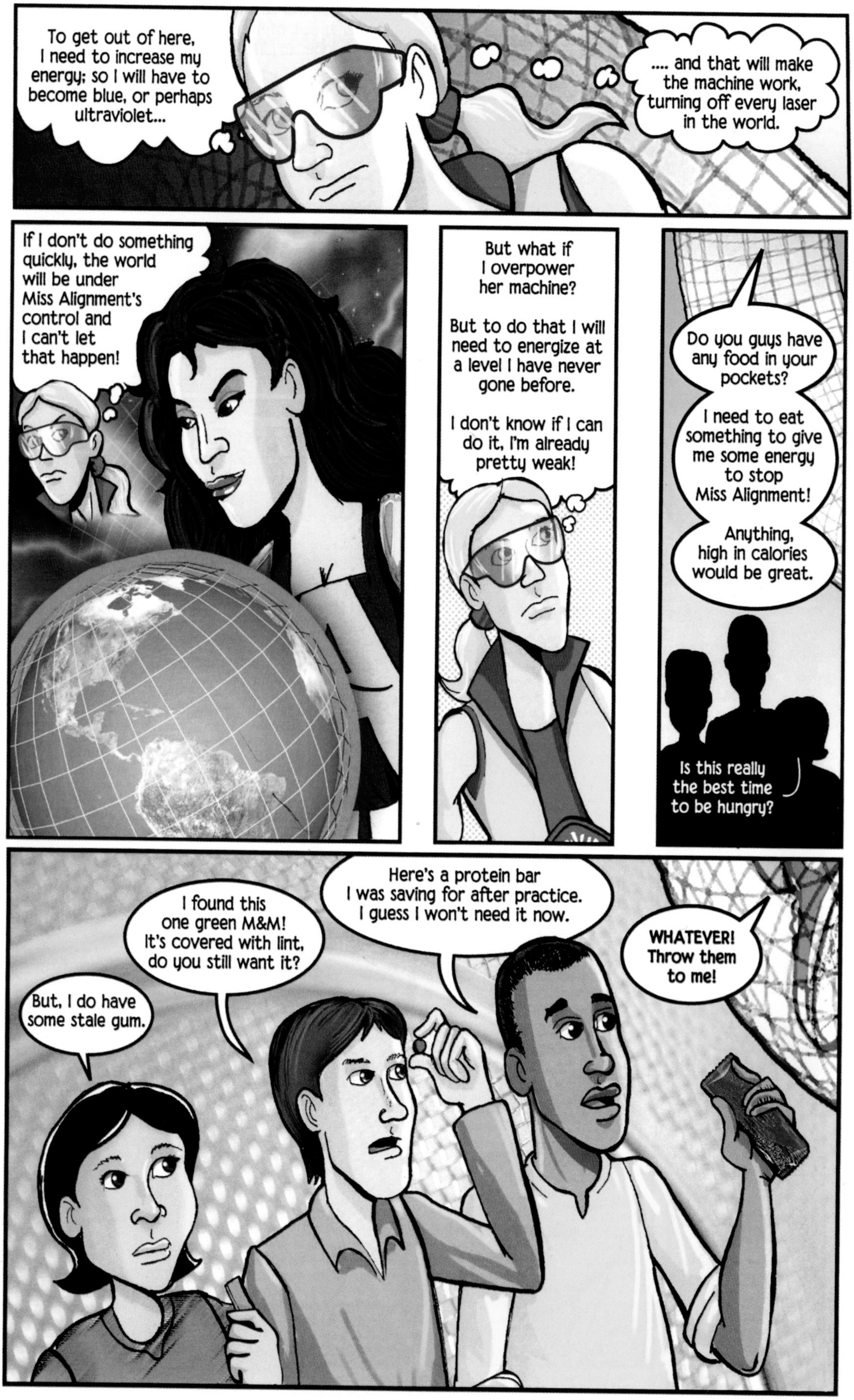
To get out of here, I need to increase my energy; so I will have to become blue, or perhaps ultraviolet...
.... and that will make the machine work, turning off every laser in the world.
If I don't do something quickly, the world will be under Miss Alignment's control and I can't let that happen!
But what if I overpower her machine?
But to do that I will need to energize at a level I have never gone before.
I don't know if I can do it, I'm already pretty weak!
Do you guys have any food in your pockets?
I need to eat something to give me some energy to stop Miss Alignment!
Anything, high in calories would be great.
Is this really the best time to be hungry?
Here's a protein bar I was saving for after practice. I guess I won't need it now.
I found this one green M&M! It's covered with lint, do you still want it?
But, I do have some stale gum.
WHATEVER! Throw them to me!

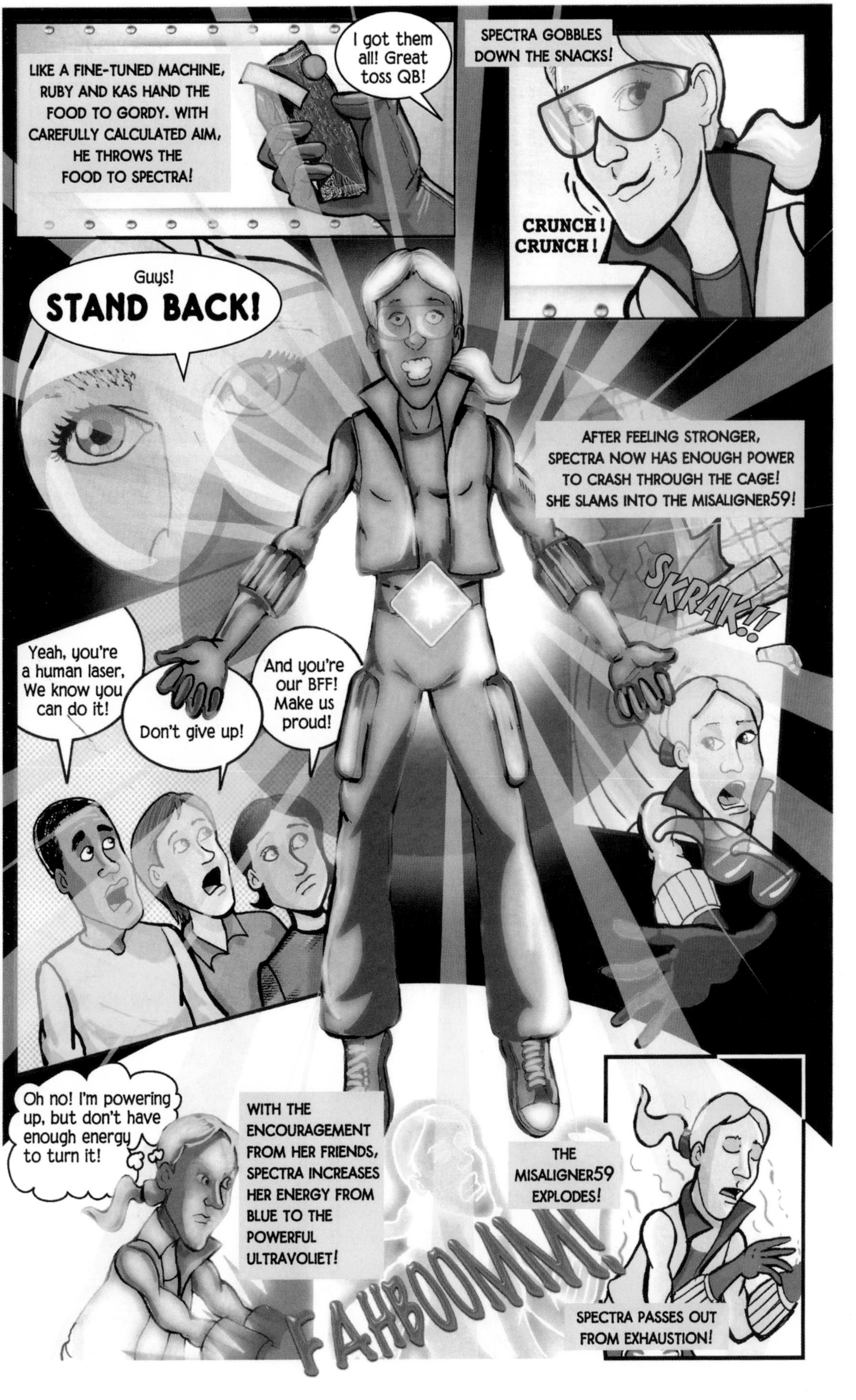
LIKE A FINE-TUNED MACHINE, RUBY AND KAS HAND THE FOOD TO GORDY. WITH CAREFULLY CALCULATED AIM, HE THROWS THE FOOD TO SPECTRA!
I got them all! Great toss QB!
SPECTRA GOBBLES DOWN THE SNACKS!
CRUNCH! CRUNCH!
Guys! STAND BACK!
AFTER FEELING STRONGER, SPECTRA NOW HAS ENOUGH POWER TO CRASH THROUGH THE CAGE! SHE SLAMS INTO THE MISALIGNER59!
SKRAK!!
Yeah, you're a human laser, We know you can do it!
Don't give up!
And you're our BFF! Make us proud!
Oh no! I'm powering up, but don't have enough energy to turn it!
WITH THE ENCOURAGEMENT FROM HER FRIENDS, SPECTRA INCREASES HER ENERGY FROM BLUE TO THE POWERFUL ULTRAVOLIET!
FAHBOOMM!
THE MISALIGNER59 EXPLODES!
SPECTRA PASSES OUT FROM EXHAUSTION!

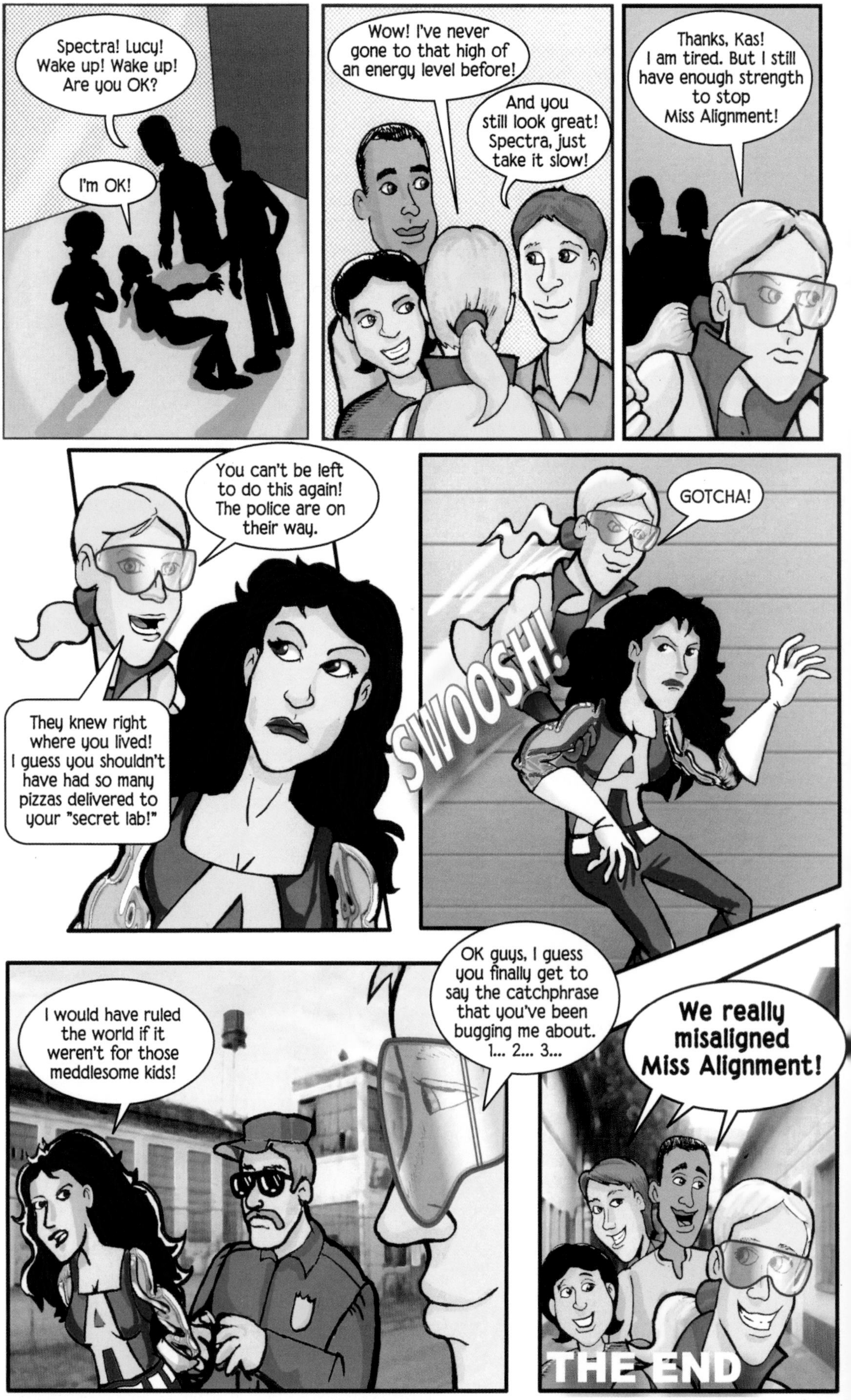
Spectra! Lucy! Wake up! Wake up! Are you OK?
I'm OK!
Wow! I've never gone to that high of an energy level before!
And you still look great! Spectra, just take it slow!
Thanks, Kas! I am tired. But I still have enough strength to stop Miss Alignment!
You can't be left to do this again! The police are on their way.
They knew right where you lived! I guess you shouldn't have had so many pizzas delivered to your "secret lab!"
GOTCHA!
SWOOSH!
I would have ruled the world if it weren't for those meddlesome kids!
OK guys, I guess you finally get to say the catchphrase that you've been bugging me about. 1... 2... 3...
We really misaligned Miss Alignment!
THE END

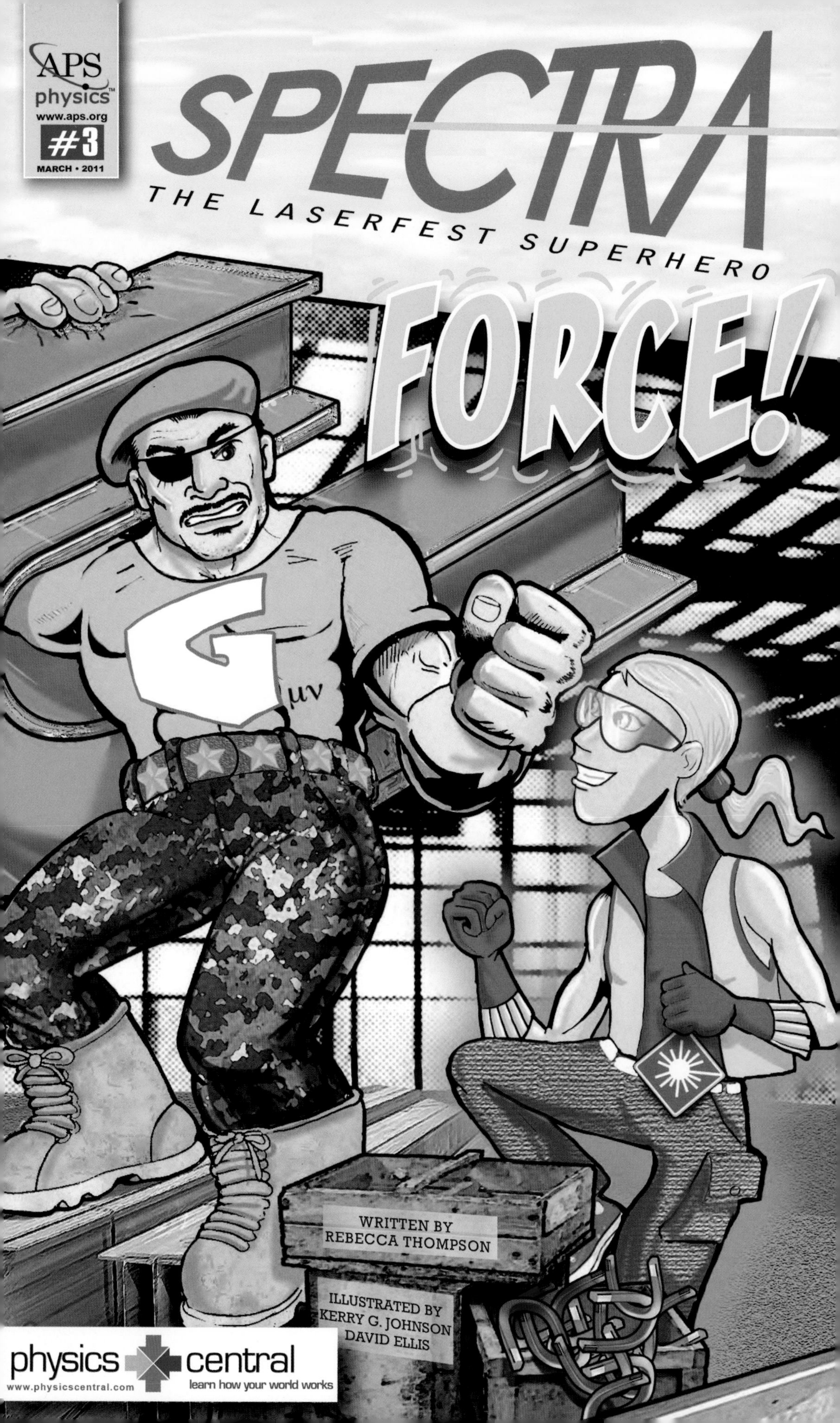
APS
physics™
www.aps.org
#3
MARCH • 2011
SPECTRA
THE LASERFEST SUPERHERO
FORCE!
G
μν
WRITTEN BY
REBECCA THOMPSON
ILLUSTRATED BY
KERRY G. JOHNSON
DAVID ELLIS
physics central
www.physicscentral.com
learn how your world works

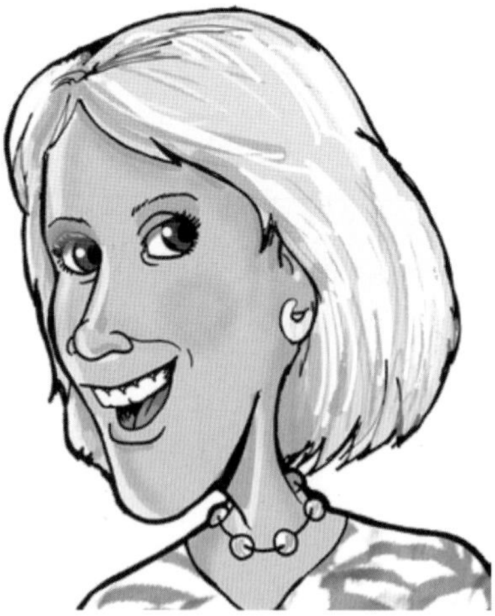

FAYE DANIEL

June 27, 1950 - December 24, 2010

DEDICATED TO MY MA,
WHO WAS THE GREATEST TEACHER
I HAVE EVER KNOWN,
BOTH IN A CLASSROOM
AND IN MY LIFE.

– Rebecca Thompson

Written by Rebecca Thompson
Art direction and coloring by Kerry G. Johnson
Illustrations by Kerry G. Johnson *(Part 1)* **and David Ellis** *(Part 2)*
Activity illustrations by Nancy Bennett-Karasik

PhysicsQuest 2010: Spectra's Force - Issue #3
is published by the American Physical Society

Library of Congress Control Number: 2011902569

Printed in the U.S.A.

SPECTRA'S FORCE

PART 1

WRITTEN BY REBECCA THOMPSON • ILLUSTRATIONS BY KERRY G. JOHNSON

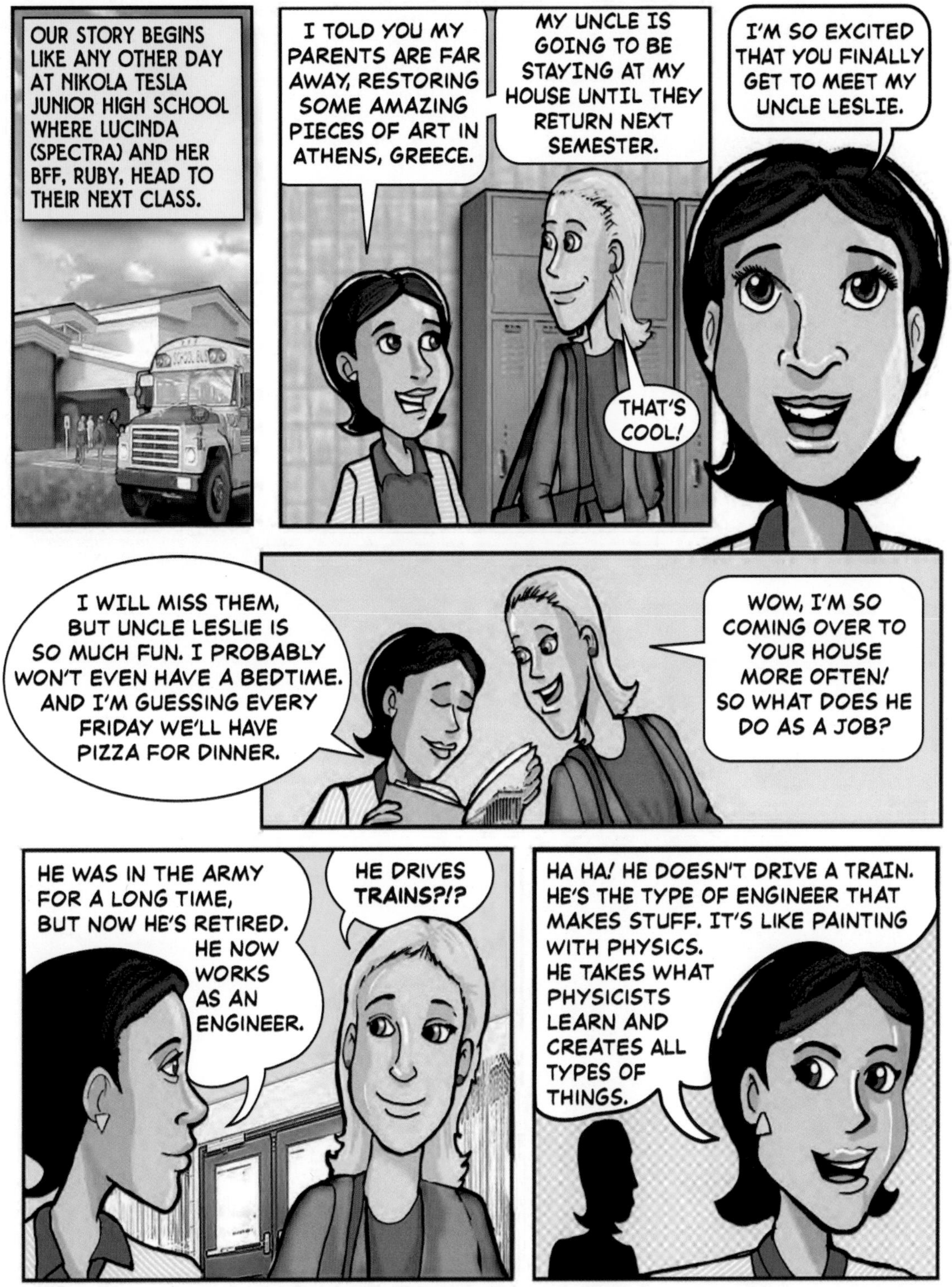
OUR STORY BEGINS LIKE ANY OTHER DAY AT NIKOLA TESLA JUNIOR HIGH SCHOOL WHERE LUCINDA (SPECTRA) AND HER BFF, RUBY, HEAD TO THEIR NEXT CLASS.
I TOLD YOU MY PARENTS ARE FAR AWAY, RESTORING SOME AMAZING PIECES OF ART IN ATHENS, GREECE.
MY UNCLE IS GOING TO BE STAYING AT MY HOUSE UNTIL THEY RETURN NEXT SEMESTER.
THAT'S COOL!
I'M SO EXCITED THAT YOU FINALLY GET TO MEET MY UNCLE LESLIE.
I WILL MISS THEM, BUT UNCLE LESLIE IS SO MUCH FUN. I PROBABLY WON'T EVEN HAVE A BEDTIME. AND I'M GUESSING EVERY FRIDAY WE'LL HAVE PIZZA FOR DINNER.
WOW, I'M SO COMING OVER TO YOUR HOUSE MORE OFTEN! SO WHAT DOES HE DO AS A JOB?
HE WAS IN THE ARMY FOR A LONG TIME, BUT NOW HE'S RETIRED. HE NOW WORKS AS AN ENGINEER.
HE DRIVES TRAINS?!?
HA HA! HE DOESN'T DRIVE A TRAIN. HE'S THE TYPE OF ENGINEER THAT MAKES STUFF. IT'S LIKE PAINTING WITH PHYSICS. HE TAKES WHAT PHYSICISTS LEARN AND CREATES ALL TYPES OF THINGS.

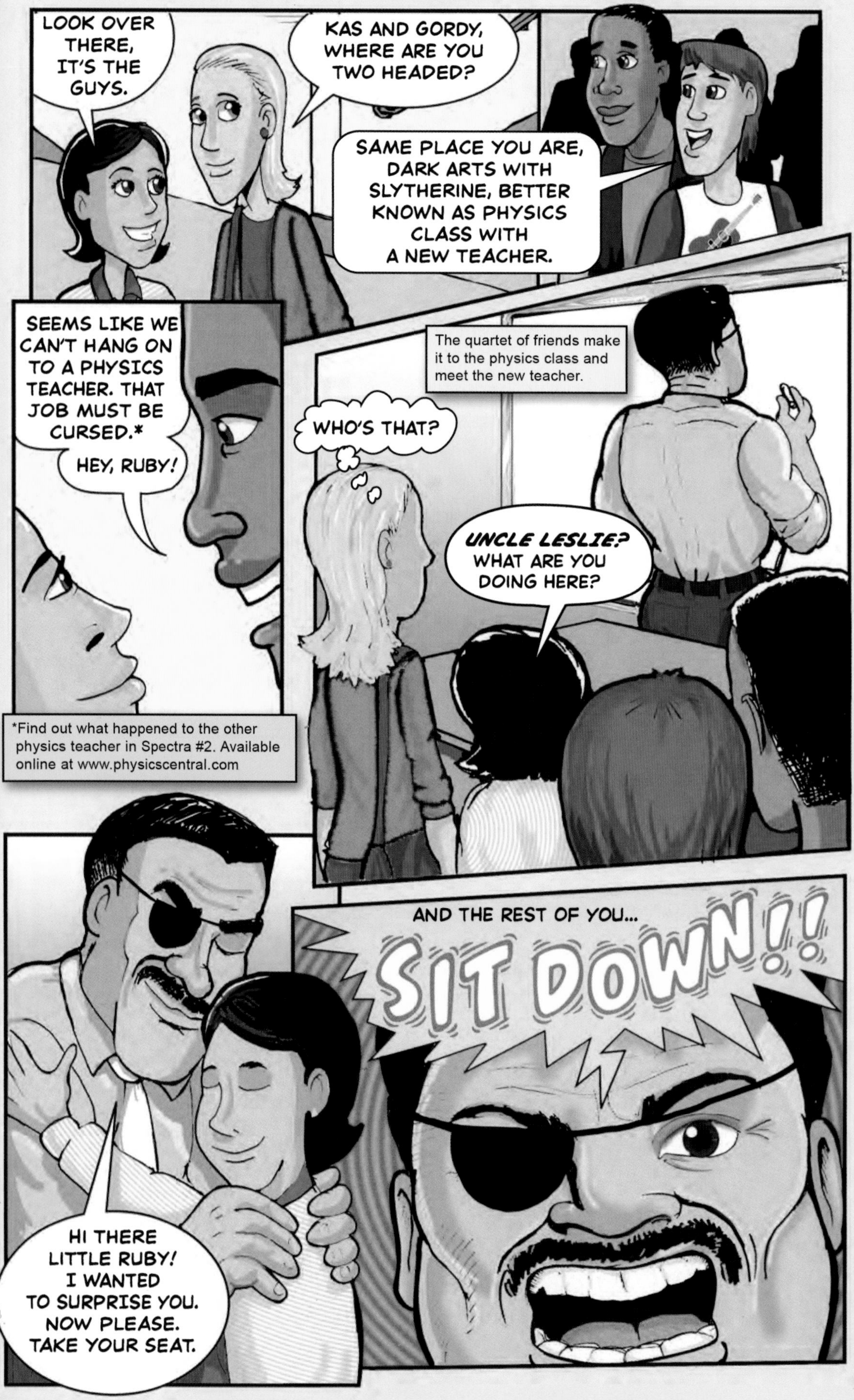
LOOK OVER THERE, IT'S THE GUYS.
KAS AND GORDY, WHERE ARE YOU TWO HEADED?
SAME PLACE YOU ARE, DARK ARTS WITH SLYTHERINE, BETTER KNOWN AS PHYSICS CLASS WITH A NEW TEACHER.
SEEMS LIKE WE CAN'T HANG ON TO A PHYSICS TEACHER. THAT JOB MUST BE CURSED.*
HEY, RUBY!
*Find out what happened to the other physics teacher in Spectra #2. Available online at www.physicscentral.com
The quartet of friends make it to the physics class and meet the new teacher.
WHO'S THAT?
UNCLE LESLIE? WHAT ARE YOU DOING HERE?
HI THERE LITTLE RUBY! I WANTED TO SURPRISE YOU. NOW PLEASE. TAKE YOUR SEAT.
AND THE REST OF YOU...
SIT DOWN!!

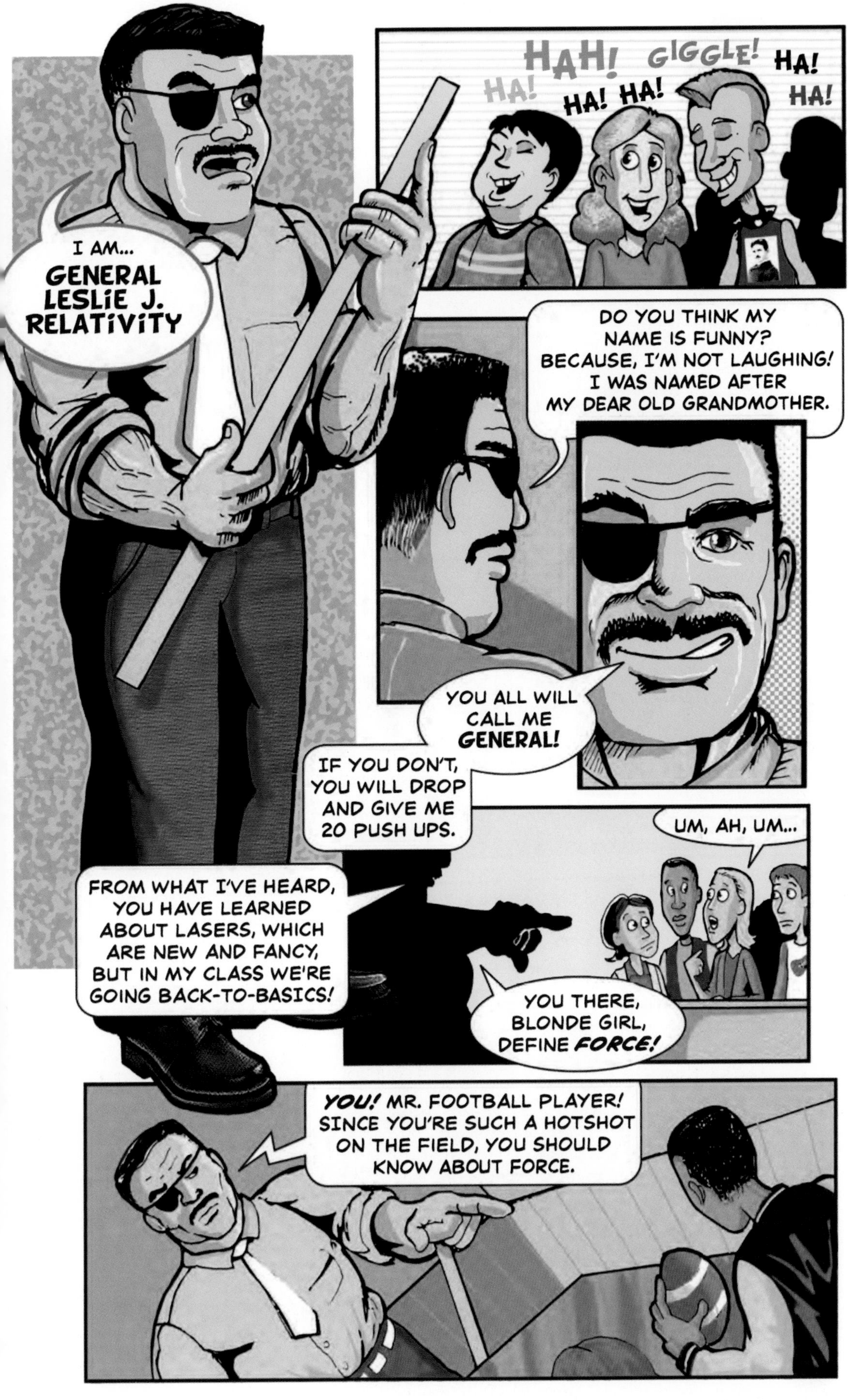
I AM...
GENERAL LESLIE J. RELATIVITY
HAH! GIGGLE! HA! HA! HA! HA! HA! HA!
DO YOU THINK MY NAME IS FUNNY? BECAUSE, I'M NOT LAUGHING! I WAS NAMED AFTER MY DEAR OLD GRANDMOTHER.
YOU ALL WILL CALL ME GENERAL!
IF YOU DON'T, YOU WILL DROP AND GIVE ME 20 PUSH UPS.
FROM WHAT I'VE HEARD, YOU HAVE LEARNED ABOUT LASERS, WHICH ARE NEW AND FANCY, BUT IN MY CLASS WE'RE GOING BACK-TO-BASICS!
YOU THERE, BLONDE GIRL, DEFINE FORCE!
UM, AH, UM...
YOU! MR. FOOTBALL PLAYER! SINCE YOU'RE SUCH A HOTSHOT ON THE FIELD, YOU SHOULD KNOW ABOUT FORCE.

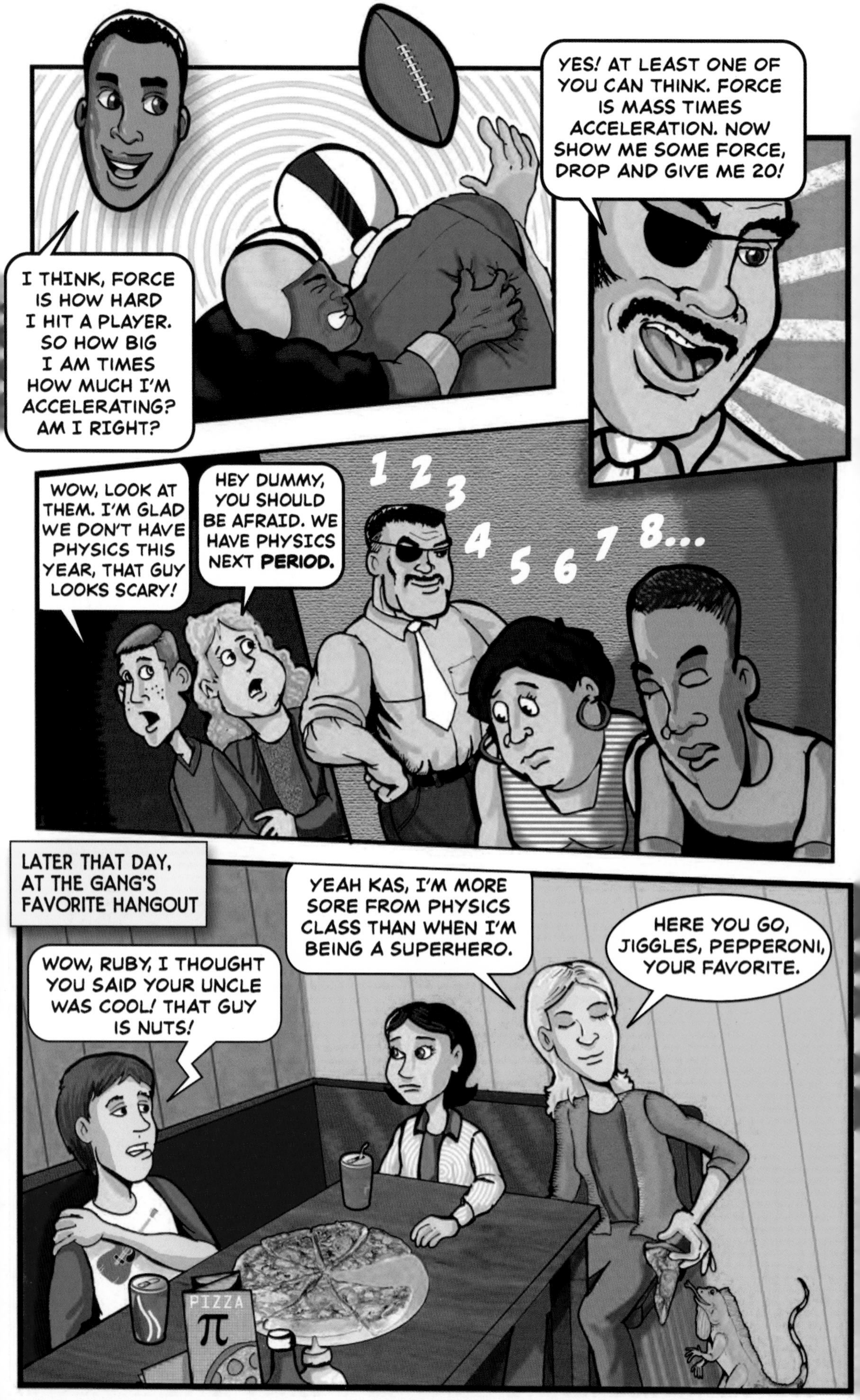
I THINK, FORCE IS HOW HARD I HIT A PLAYER. SO HOW BIG I AM TIMES HOW MUCH I'M ACCELERATING? AM I RIGHT?
YES! AT LEAST ONE OF YOU CAN THINK. FORCE IS MASS TIMES ACCELERATION. NOW SHOW ME SOME FORCE, DROP AND GIVE ME 20!
WOW, LOOK AT THEM. I'M GLAD WE DON'T HAVE PHYSICS THIS YEAR, THAT GUY LOOKS SCARY!
HEY DUMMY, YOU SHOULD BE AFRAID. WE HAVE PHYSICS NEXT PERIOD.
1 2 3 4 5 6 7 8...
LATER THAT DAY, AT THE GANG'S FAVORITE HANGOUT
WOW, RUBY, I THOUGHT YOU SAID YOUR UNCLE WAS COOL! THAT GUY IS NUTS!
YEAH KAS, I'M MORE SORE FROM PHYSICS CLASS THAN WHEN I'M BEING A SUPERHERO.
HERE YOU GO, JIGGLES, PEPPERONI, YOUR FAVORITE.
PIZZA
π

I'M REALLY SORRY GUYS, HE'S ALWAYS BEEN SO GREAT TO ME. THE LAST TIME HE WAS HERE, HE LET ME STAY UP LATE AND WE PLAYED WITH MY GLOW IN THE DARK PAINT AND LASERS.

NEXT TIME YOU SEE GLOW IN THE DARK PAINT, I'LL SHOW YOU HOW TO HAVE SOME FUN WITH IT.

THEN WE USED MY MODELING CLAY AND SOME PIE PANS TO "TEST GRAVITY." HE MADE SCIENCE SO MUCH FUN. I THINK YOU GUYS ARE BEING TOO HARSH! I HAD FUN TODAY.

KAS, GET OFF RUBY'S CASE! THE GENERAL TAUGHT ME A LOT ABOUT FOOTBALL AND PHYSICS.

YEAH, BECAUSE YOU'RE THE ONLY ONE WHO DOESN'T HAVE TO ICE WHEN YOU GET HOME!

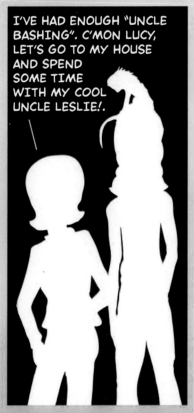

I'VE HAD ENOUGH "UNCLE BASHING". C'MON LUCY, LET'S GO TO MY HOUSE AND SPEND SOME TIME WITH MY COOL UNCLE LESLIE!.

UNCLE LESLIE? I'M HOME AND I BROUGHT MY FRIEND LUCINDA.

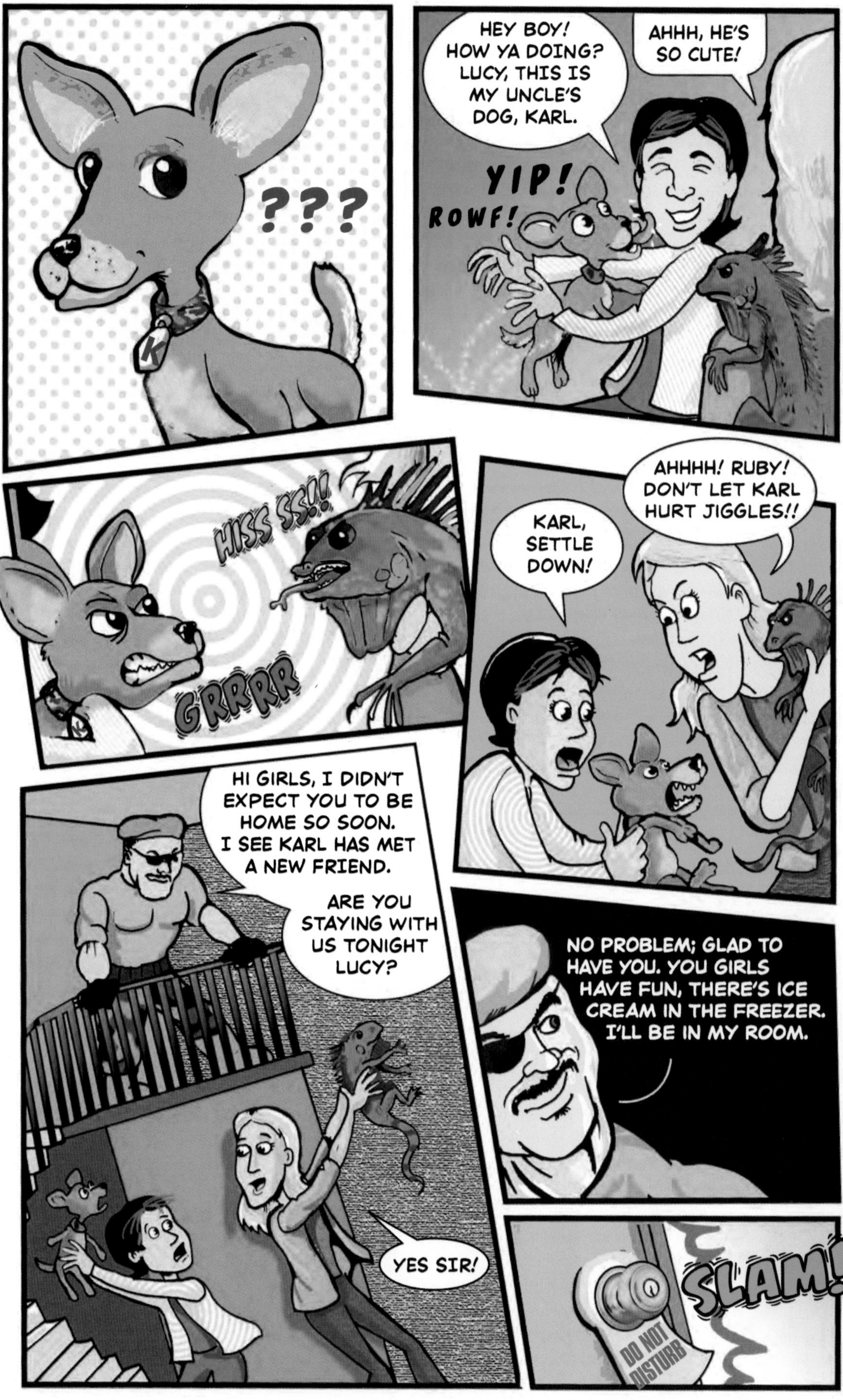
???
HEY BOY! HOW YA DOING? LUCY, THIS IS MY UNCLE'S DOG, KARL.
AHHH, HE'S SO CUTE!
YIP!
ROWF!
HISSSSS!!
GRRRR
KARL, SETTLE DOWN!
AHHHH! RUBY! DON'T LET KARL HURT JIGGLES!!
HI GIRLS, I DIDN'T EXPECT YOU TO BE HOME SO SOON. I SEE KARL HAS MET A NEW FRIEND.
ARE YOU STAYING WITH US TONIGHT LUCY?
YES SIR!
NO PROBLEM; GLAD TO HAVE YOU. YOU GIRLS HAVE FUN, THERE'S ICE CREAM IN THE FREEZER. I'LL BE IN MY ROOM.
SLAM!
DO NOT DISTURB

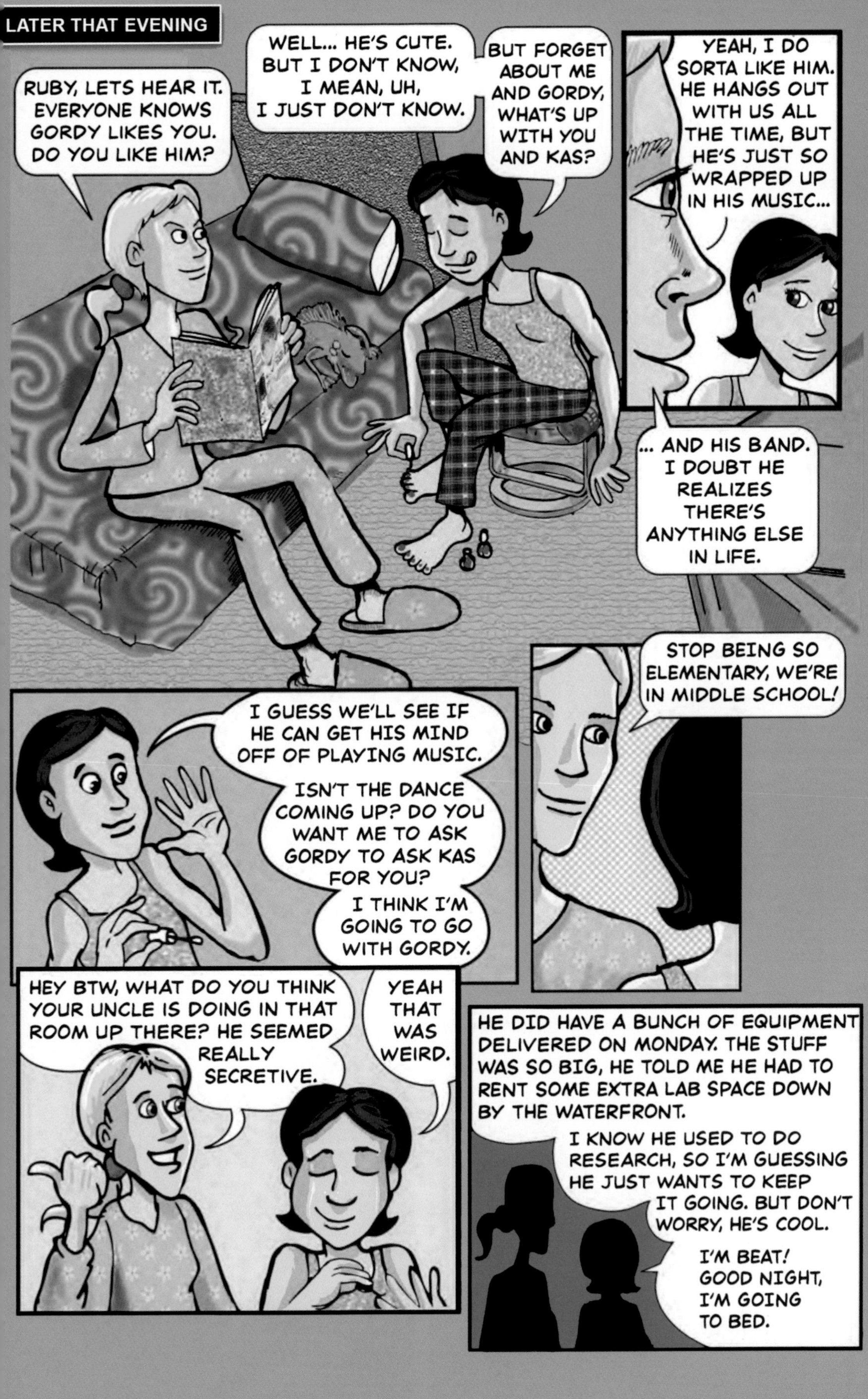
LATER THAT EVENING
RUBY, LETS HEAR IT. EVERYONE KNOWS GORDY LIKES YOU. DO YOU LIKE HIM?
WELL... HE'S CUTE. BUT I DON'T KNOW, I MEAN, UH, I JUST DON'T KNOW.
BUT FORGET ABOUT ME AND GORDY, WHAT'S UP WITH YOU AND KAS?
YEAH, I DO SORTA LIKE HIM. HE HANGS OUT WITH US ALL THE TIME, BUT HE'S JUST SO WRAPPED UP IN HIS MUSIC...
... AND HIS BAND. I DOUBT HE REALIZES THERE'S ANYTHING ELSE IN LIFE.
I GUESS WE'LL SEE IF HE CAN GET HIS MIND OFF OF PLAYING MUSIC.
ISN'T THE DANCE COMING UP? DO YOU WANT ME TO ASK GORDY TO ASK KAS FOR YOU?
I THINK I'M GOING TO GO WITH GORDY.
STOP BEING SO ELEMENTARY, WE'RE IN MIDDLE SCHOOL!
HEY BTW, WHAT DO YOU THINK YOUR UNCLE IS DOING IN THAT ROOM UP THERE? HE SEEMED REALLY SECRETIVE.
YEAH THAT WAS WEIRD.
HE DID HAVE A BUNCH OF EQUIPMENT DELIVERED ON MONDAY. THE STUFF WAS SO BIG, HE TOLD ME HE HAD TO RENT SOME EXTRA LAB SPACE DOWN BY THE WATERFRONT.
I KNOW HE USED TO DO RESEARCH, SO I'M GUESSING HE JUST WANTS TO KEEP IT GOING. BUT DON'T WORRY, HE'S COOL.
I'M BEAT! GOOD NIGHT, I'M GOING TO BED.

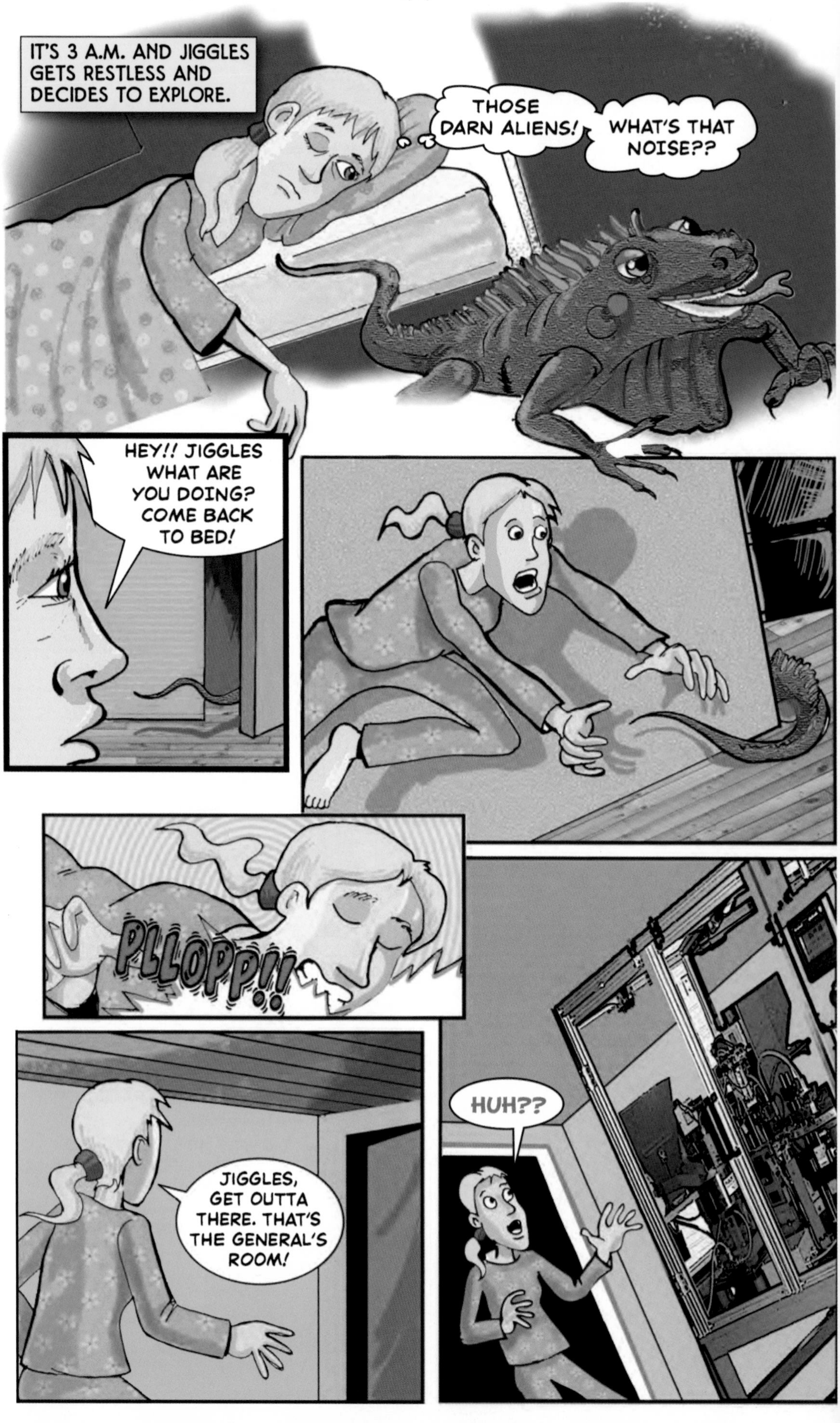
IT'S 3 A.M. AND JIGGLES GETS RESTLESS AND DECIDES TO EXPLORE.
THOSE DARN ALIENS!
WHAT'S THAT NOISE??
HEY!! JIGGLES WHAT ARE YOU DOING? COME BACK TO BED!
PLLOPP!!
JIGGLES, GET OUTTA THERE. THAT'S THE GENERAL'S ROOM!
HUH??

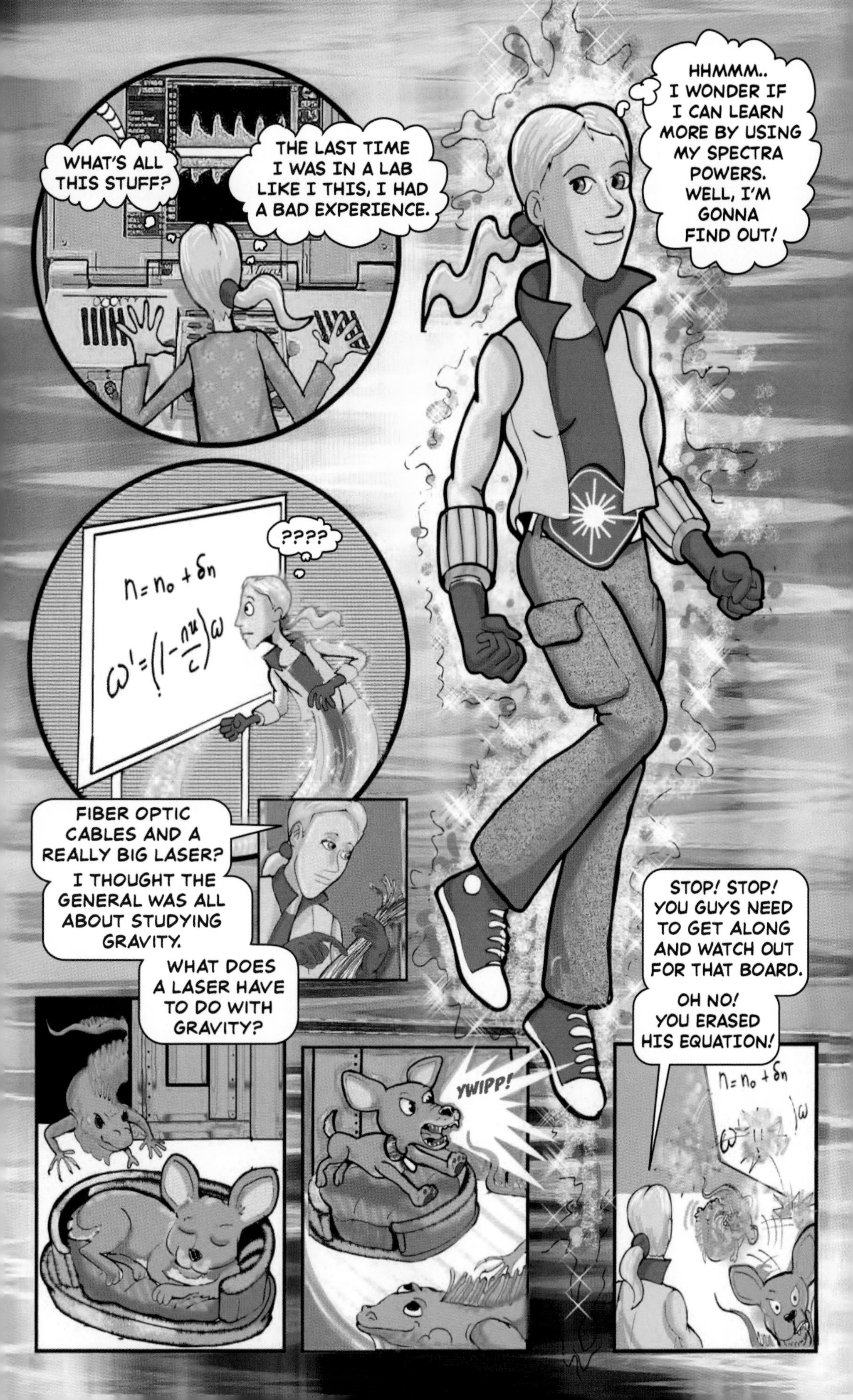
WHAT'S ALL THIS STUFF?
THE LAST TIME I WAS IN A LAB LIKE I THIS, I HAD A BAD EXPERIENCE.
HHMMM.. I WONDER IF I CAN LEARN MORE BY USING MY SPECTRA POWERS. WELL, I'M GONNA FIND OUT!
????
FIBER OPTIC CABLES AND A REALLY BIG LASER?
I THOUGHT THE GENERAL WAS ALL ABOUT STUDYING GRAVITY.
WHAT DOES A LASER HAVE TO DO WITH GRAVITY?
YWIPP!
STOP! STOP! YOU GUYS NEED TO GET ALONG AND WATCH OUT FOR THAT BOARD.
OH NO! YOU ERASED HIS EQUATION!

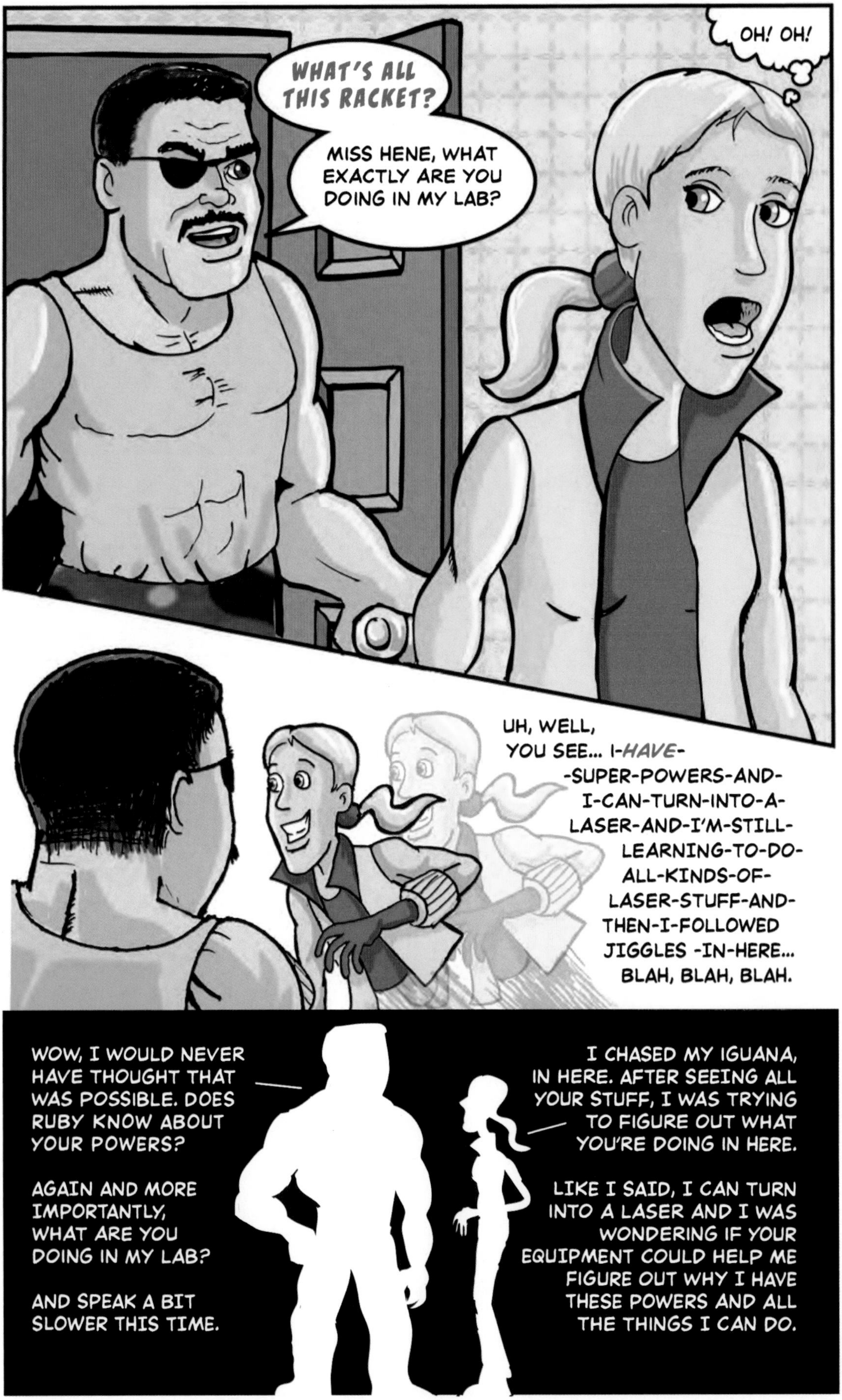
OH! OH!
WHAT'S ALL THIS RACKET?
MISS HENE, WHAT EXACTLY ARE YOU DOING IN MY LAB?
UH, WELL, YOU SEE... I-HAVE-
-SUPER-POWERS-AND-I-CAN-TURN-INTO-A-LASER-AND-I'M-STILL-LEARNING-TO-DO-ALL-KINDS-OF-LASER-STUFF-AND-THEN-I-FOLLOWED JIGGLES -IN-HERE... BLAH, BLAH, BLAH.
WOW, I WOULD NEVER HAVE THOUGHT THAT WAS POSSIBLE. DOES RUBY KNOW ABOUT YOUR POWERS?
AGAIN AND MORE IMPORTANTLY, WHAT ARE YOU DOING IN MY LAB?
AND SPEAK A BIT SLOWER THIS TIME.
I CHASED MY IGUANA, IN HERE. AFTER SEEING ALL YOUR STUFF, I WAS TRYING TO FIGURE OUT WHAT YOU'RE DOING IN HERE.
LIKE I SAID, I CAN TURN INTO A LASER AND I WAS WONDERING IF YOUR EQUIPMENT COULD HELP ME FIGURE OUT WHY I HAVE THESE POWERS AND ALL THE THINGS I CAN DO.

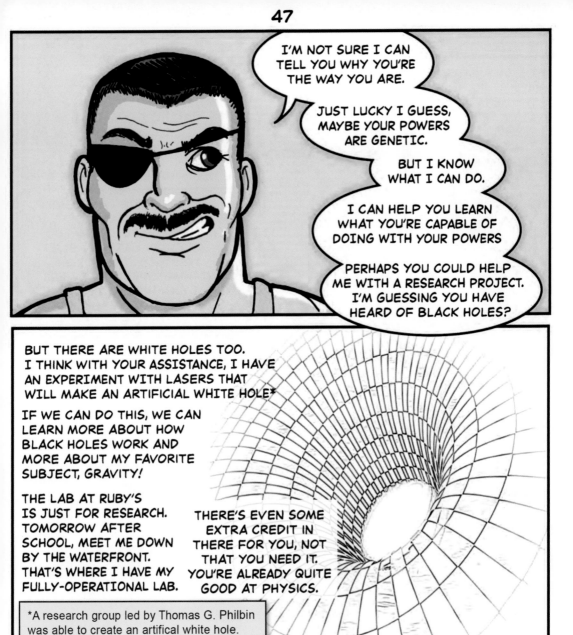

I'M NOT SURE I CAN TELL YOU WHY YOU'RE THE WAY YOU ARE.

JUST LUCKY I GUESS, MAYBE YOUR POWERS ARE GENETIC.

BUT I KNOW WHAT I CAN DO.

I CAN HELP YOU LEARN WHAT YOU'RE CAPABLE OF DOING WITH YOUR POWERS

PERHAPS YOU COULD HELP ME WITH A RESEARCH PROJECT. I'M GUESSING YOU HAVE HEARD OF BLACK HOLES?

BUT THERE ARE WHITE HOLES TOO. I THINK WITH YOUR ASSISTANCE, I HAVE AN EXPERIMENT WITH LASERS THAT WILL MAKE AN ARTIFICIAL WHITE HOLE*

IF WE CAN DO THIS, WE CAN LEARN MORE ABOUT HOW BLACK HOLES WORK AND MORE ABOUT MY FAVORITE SUBJECT, GRAVITY!

THE LAB AT RUBY'S IS JUST FOR RESEARCH. TOMORROW AFTER SCHOOL, MEET ME DOWN BY THE WATERFRONT. THAT'S WHERE I HAVE MY FULLY-OPERATIONAL LAB.

THERE'S EVEN SOME EXTRA CREDIT IN THERE FOR YOU, NOT THAT YOU NEED IT. YOU'RE ALREADY QUITE GOOD AT PHYSICS.

*A research group led by Thomas G. Philbin was able to create an artifical white hole.

THE NEXT DAY BACK AT SCHOOL

OH, LOOKS LIKE THE BIG DANCE IS COMING UP. I'M NOT A GREAT DANCER, BUT WOULDN'T MIND GOING.

GORDY'S TAKING RUBY.

MAYBE WE CAN GO TOGETHER? WHAT DO YOU THINK?

YES! WHAT TOOK YOU SO LONG?

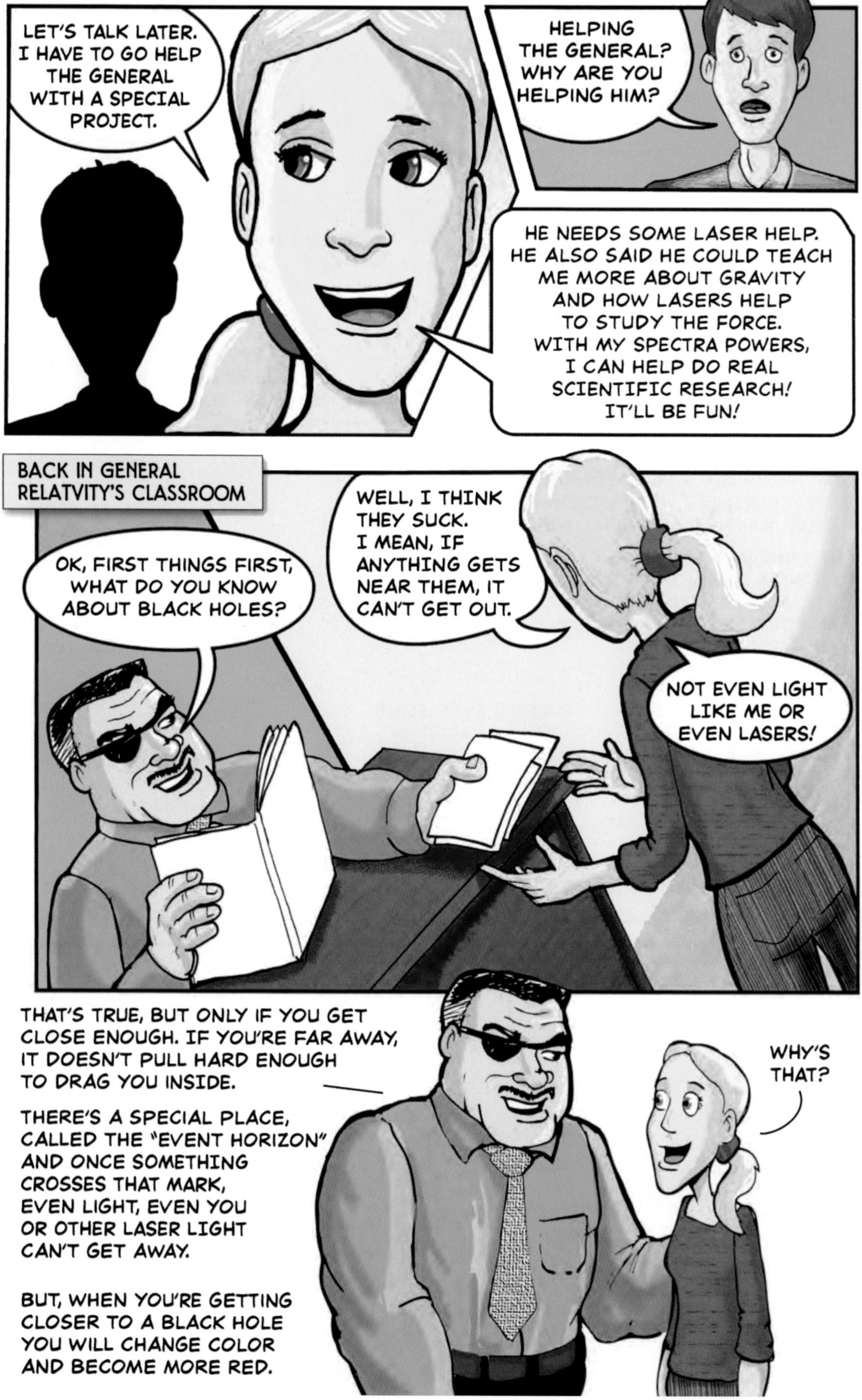
LET'S TALK LATER. I HAVE TO GO HELP THE GENERAL WITH A SPECIAL PROJECT.
HELPING THE GENERAL? WHY ARE YOU HELPING HIM?
HE NEEDS SOME LASER HELP. HE ALSO SAID HE COULD TEACH ME MORE ABOUT GRAVITY AND HOW LASERS HELP TO STUDY THE FORCE. WITH MY SPECTRA POWERS, I CAN HELP DO REAL SCIENTIFIC RESEARCH! IT'LL BE FUN!
BACK IN GENERAL RELATVITY'S CLASSROOM
OK, FIRST THINGS FIRST, WHAT DO YOU KNOW ABOUT BLACK HOLES?
WELL, I THINK THEY SUCK. I MEAN, IF ANYTHING GETS NEAR THEM, IT CAN'T GET OUT.
NOT EVEN LIGHT LIKE ME OR EVEN LASERS!
THAT'S TRUE, BUT ONLY IF YOU GET CLOSE ENOUGH. IF YOU'RE FAR AWAY, IT DOESN'T PULL HARD ENOUGH TO DRAG YOU INSIDE.
THERE'S A SPECIAL PLACE, CALLED THE "EVENT HORIZON" AND ONCE SOMETHING CROSSES THAT MARK, EVEN LIGHT, EVEN YOU OR OTHER LASER LIGHT CAN'T GET AWAY.
BUT, WHEN YOU'RE GETTING CLOSER TO A BLACK HOLE YOU WILL CHANGE COLOR AND BECOME MORE RED.
WHY'S THAT?

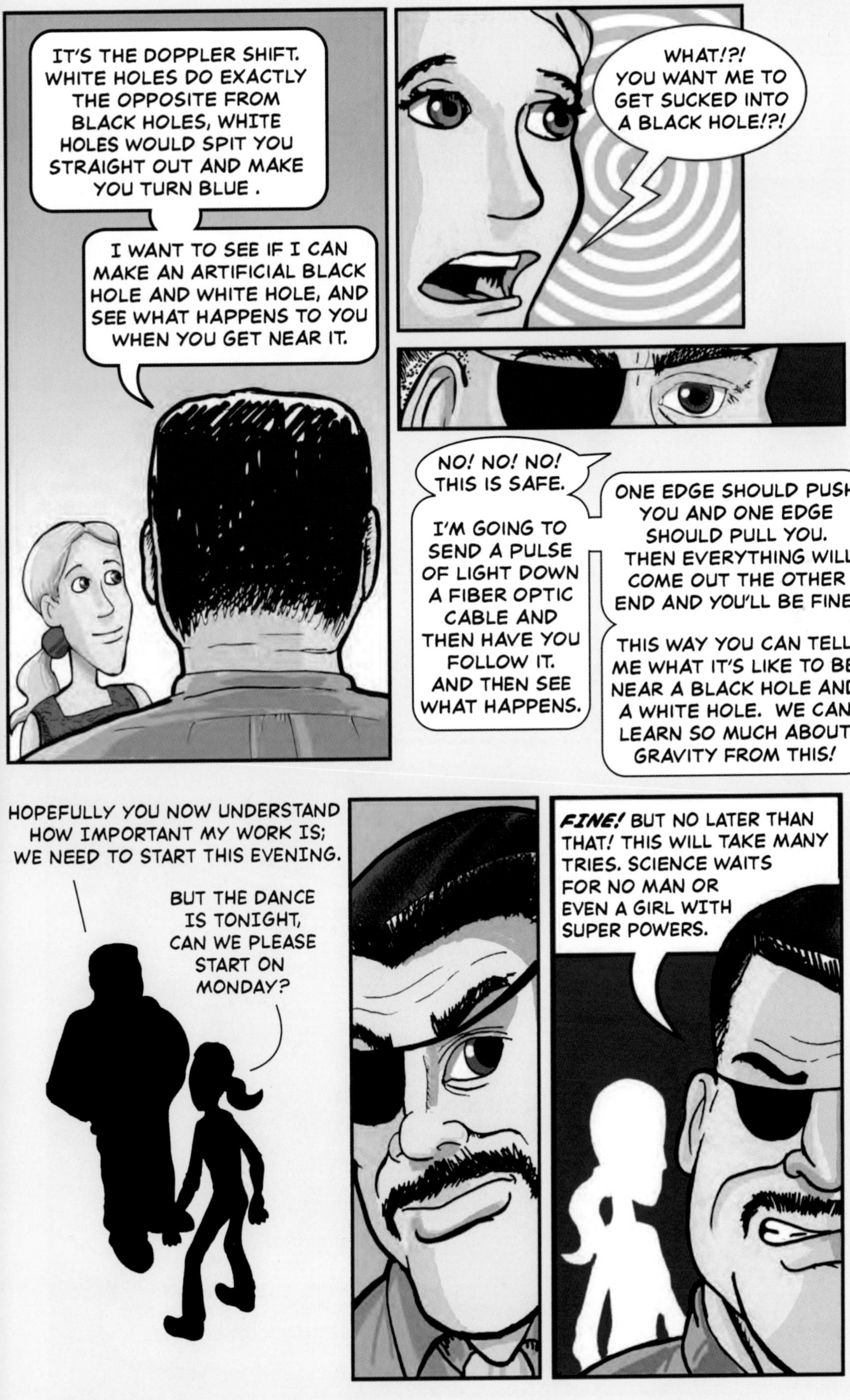
IT'S THE DOPPLER SHIFT. WHITE HOLES DO EXACTLY THE OPPOSITE FROM BLACK HOLES, WHITE HOLES WOULD SPIT YOU STRAIGHT OUT AND MAKE YOU TURN BLUE .
I WANT TO SEE IF I CAN MAKE AN ARTIFICIAL BLACK HOLE AND WHITE HOLE, AND SEE WHAT HAPPENS TO YOU WHEN YOU GET NEAR IT.
WHAT!?! YOU WANT ME TO GET SUCKED INTO A BLACK HOLE!?!
NO! NO! NO! THIS IS SAFE.
I'M GOING TO SEND A PULSE OF LIGHT DOWN A FIBER OPTIC CABLE AND THEN HAVE YOU FOLLOW IT. AND THEN SEE WHAT HAPPENS.
ONE EDGE SHOULD PUSH YOU AND ONE EDGE SHOULD PULL YOU. THEN EVERYTHING WILL COME OUT THE OTHER END AND YOU'LL BE FINE.
THIS WAY YOU CAN TELL ME WHAT IT'S LIKE TO BE NEAR A BLACK HOLE AND A WHITE HOLE. WE CAN LEARN SO MUCH ABOUT GRAVITY FROM THIS!
HOPEFULLY YOU NOW UNDERSTAND HOW IMPORTANT MY WORK IS; WE NEED TO START THIS EVENING.
BUT THE DANCE IS TONIGHT, CAN WE PLEASE START ON MONDAY?
FINE! BUT NO LATER THAN THAT! THIS WILL TAKE MANY TRIES. SCIENCE WAITS FOR NO MAN OR EVEN A GIRL WITH SUPER POWERS.

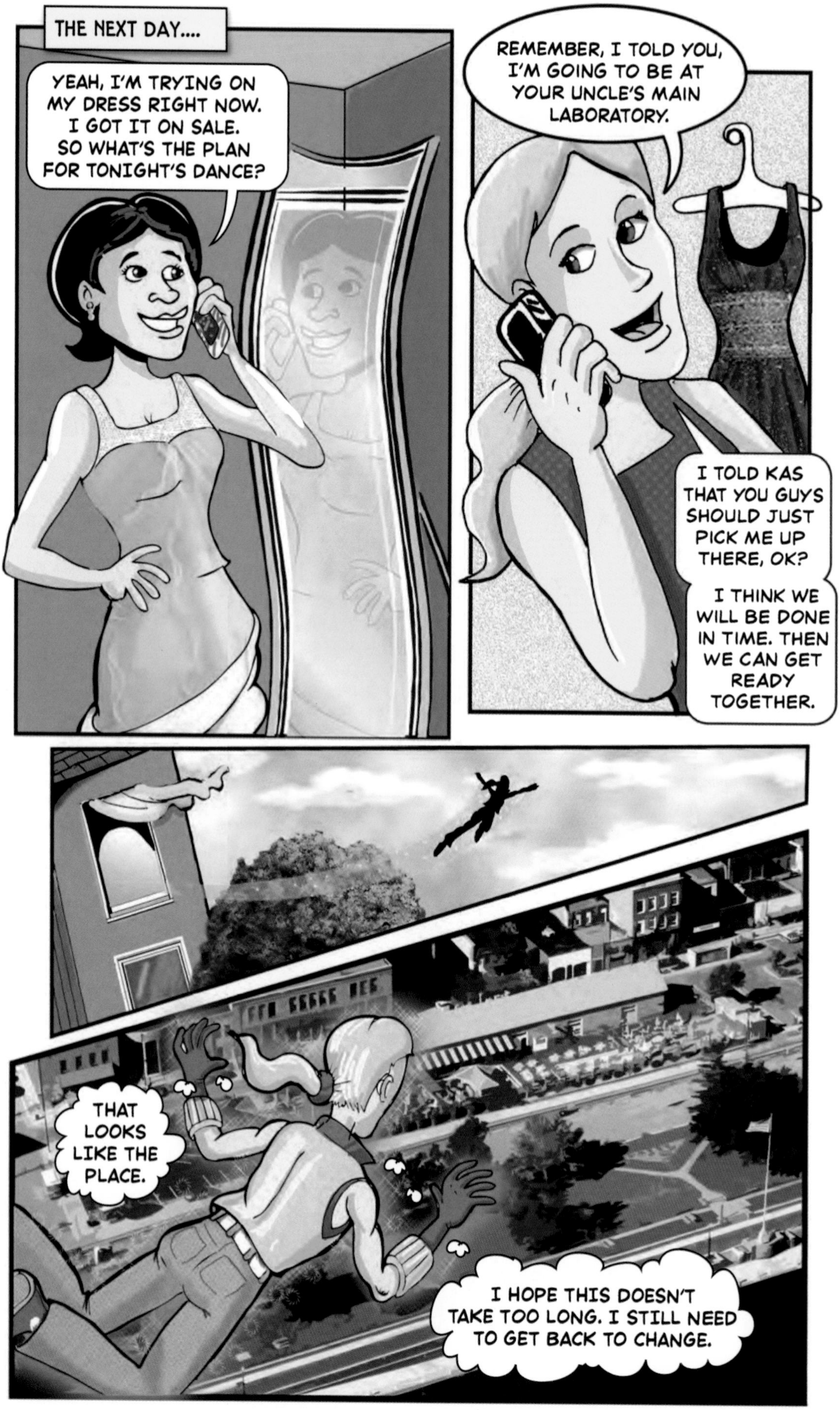
THE NEXT DAY....
YEAH, I'M TRYING ON MY DRESS RIGHT NOW. I GOT IT ON SALE. SO WHAT'S THE PLAN FOR TONIGHT'S DANCE?
REMEMBER, I TOLD YOU, I'M GOING TO BE AT YOUR UNCLE'S MAIN LABORATORY.
I TOLD KAS THAT YOU GUYS SHOULD JUST PICK ME UP THERE, OK?
I THINK WE WILL BE DONE IN TIME. THEN WE CAN GET READY TOGETHER.
THAT LOOKS LIKE THE PLACE.
I HOPE THIS DOESN'T TAKE TOO LONG. I STILL NEED TO GET BACK TO CHANGE.

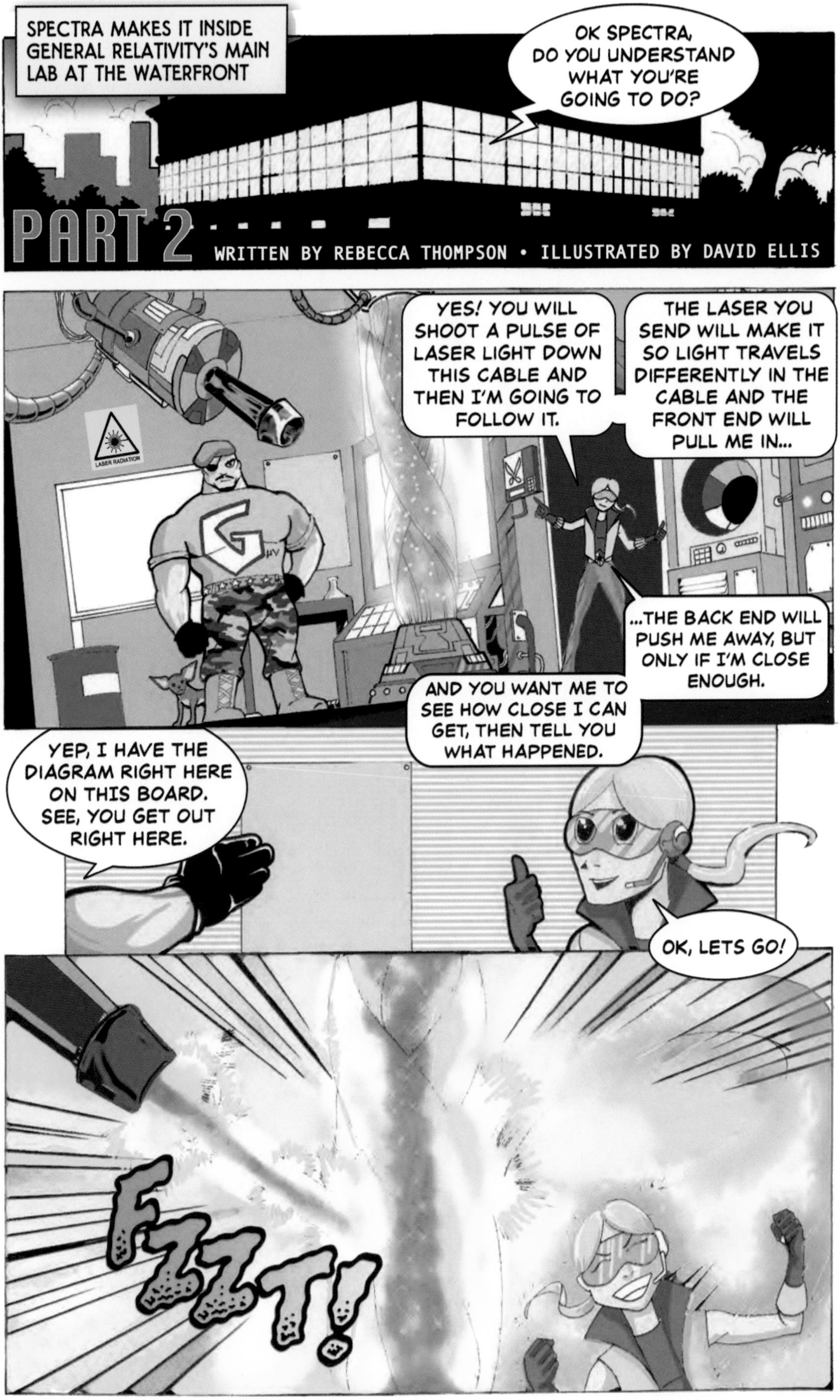
SPECTRA MAKES IT INSIDE GENERAL RELATIVITY'S MAIN LAB AT THE WATERFRONT
OK SPECTRA, DO YOU UNDERSTAND WHAT YOU'RE GOING TO DO?
PART 2
WRITTEN BY REBECCA THOMPSON • ILLUSTRATED BY DAVID ELLIS
YES! YOU WILL SHOOT A PULSE OF LASER LIGHT DOWN THIS CABLE AND THEN I'M GOING TO FOLLOW IT.
THE LASER YOU SEND WILL MAKE IT SO LIGHT TRAVELS DIFFERENTLY IN THE CABLE AND THE FRONT END WILL PULL ME IN...
...THE BACK END WILL PUSH ME AWAY, BUT ONLY IF I'M CLOSE ENOUGH.
AND YOU WANT ME TO SEE HOW CLOSE I CAN GET, THEN TELL YOU WHAT HAPPENED.
YEP, I HAVE THE DIAGRAM RIGHT HERE ON THIS BOARD. SEE, YOU GET OUT RIGHT HERE.
OK, LETS GO!
FZZZT!

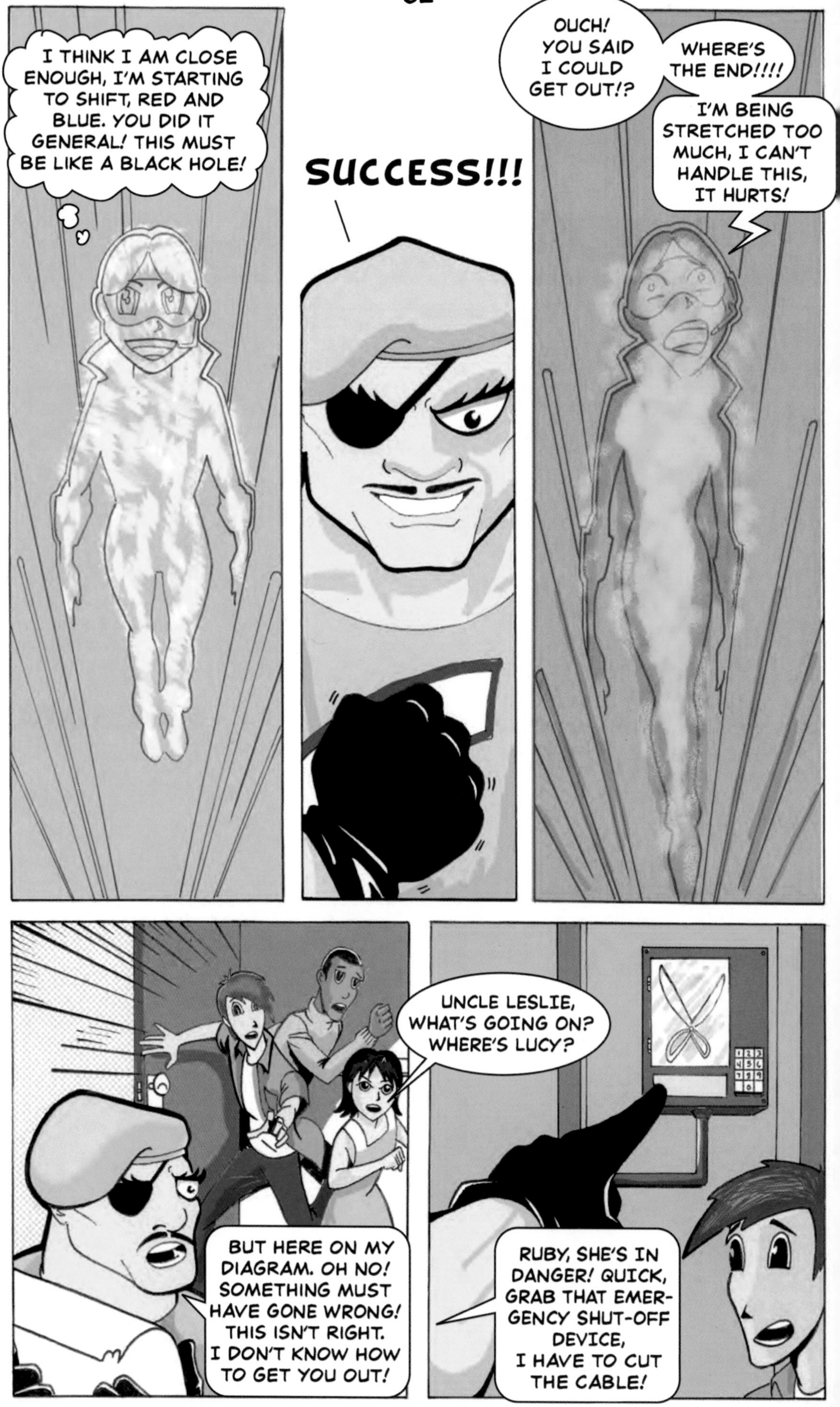
I THINK I AM CLOSE ENOUGH, I'M STARTING TO SHIFT, RED AND BLUE. YOU DID IT GENERAL! THIS MUST BE LIKE A BLACK HOLE!
SUCCESS!!!
OUCH! YOU SAID I COULD GET OUT!?
WHERE'S THE END!!!!
I'M BEING STRETCHED TOO MUCH, I CAN'T HANDLE THIS, IT HURTS!
UNCLE LESLIE, WHAT'S GOING ON? WHERE'S LUCY?
BUT HERE ON MY DIAGRAM. OH NO! SOMETHING MUST HAVE GONE WRONG! THIS ISN'T RIGHT. I DON'T KNOW HOW TO GET YOU OUT!
RUBY, SHE'S IN DANGER! QUICK, GRAB THAT EMERGENCY SHUT-OFF DEVICE, I HAVE TO CUT THE CABLE!

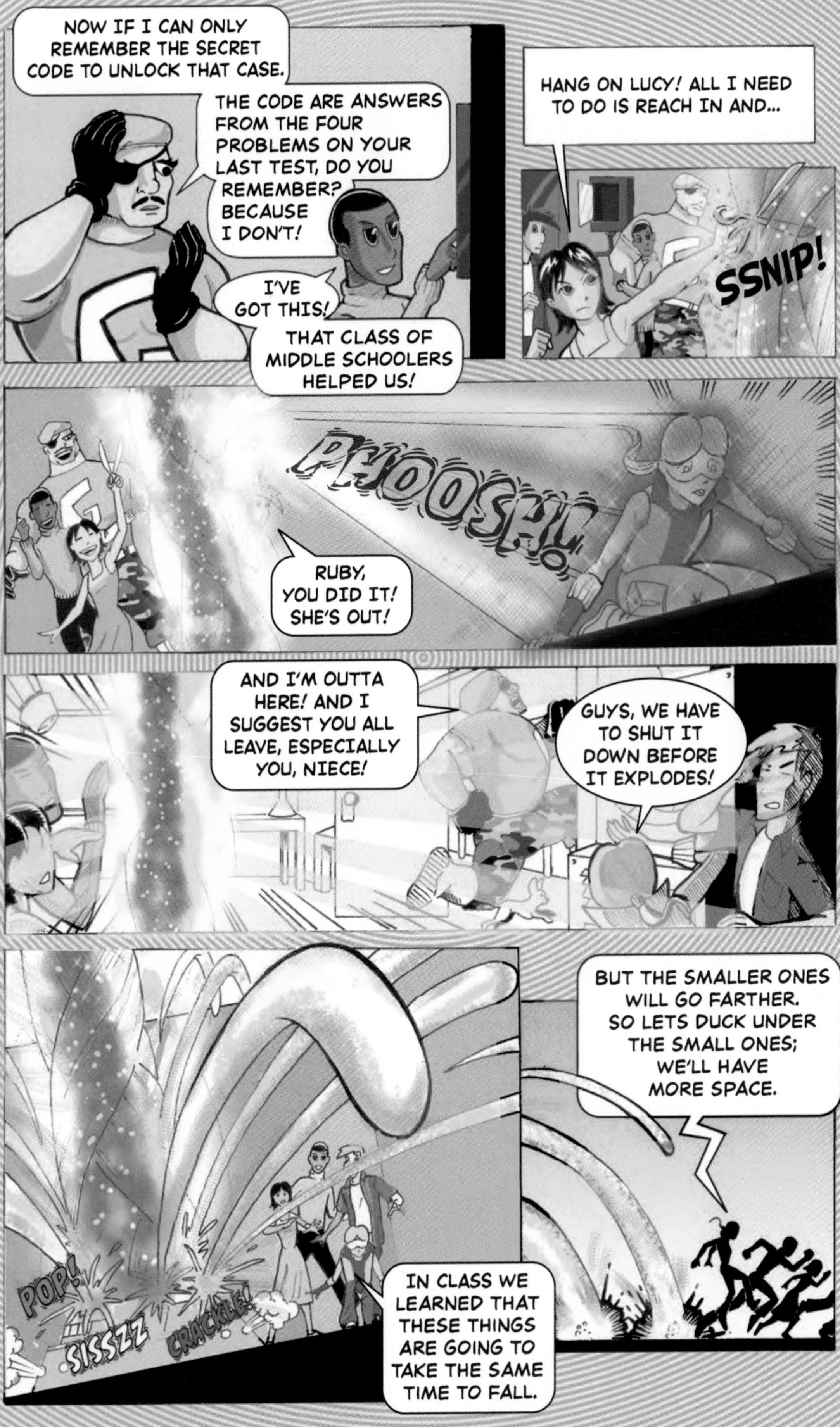
NOW IF I CAN ONLY REMEMBER THE SECRET CODE TO UNLOCK THAT CASE.
THE CODE ARE ANSWERS FROM THE FOUR PROBLEMS ON YOUR LAST TEST, DO YOU REMEMBER? BECAUSE I DON'T!
I'VE GOT THIS!
THAT CLASS OF MIDDLE SCHOOLERS HELPED US!
HANG ON LUCY! ALL I NEED TO DO IS REACH IN AND...
SSNIP!
PHOOSH!
RUBY, YOU DID IT! SHE'S OUT!
AND I'M OUTTA HERE! AND I SUGGEST YOU ALL LEAVE, ESPECIALLY YOU, NIECE!
GUYS, WE HAVE TO SHUT IT DOWN BEFORE IT EXPLODES!
POP!
SISSZZ
CRACKLE!
IN CLASS WE LEARNED THAT THESE THINGS ARE GOING TO TAKE THE SAME TIME TO FALL.
BUT THE SMALLER ONES WILL GO FARTHER. SO LETS DUCK UNDER THE SMALL ONES; WE'LL HAVE MORE SPACE.

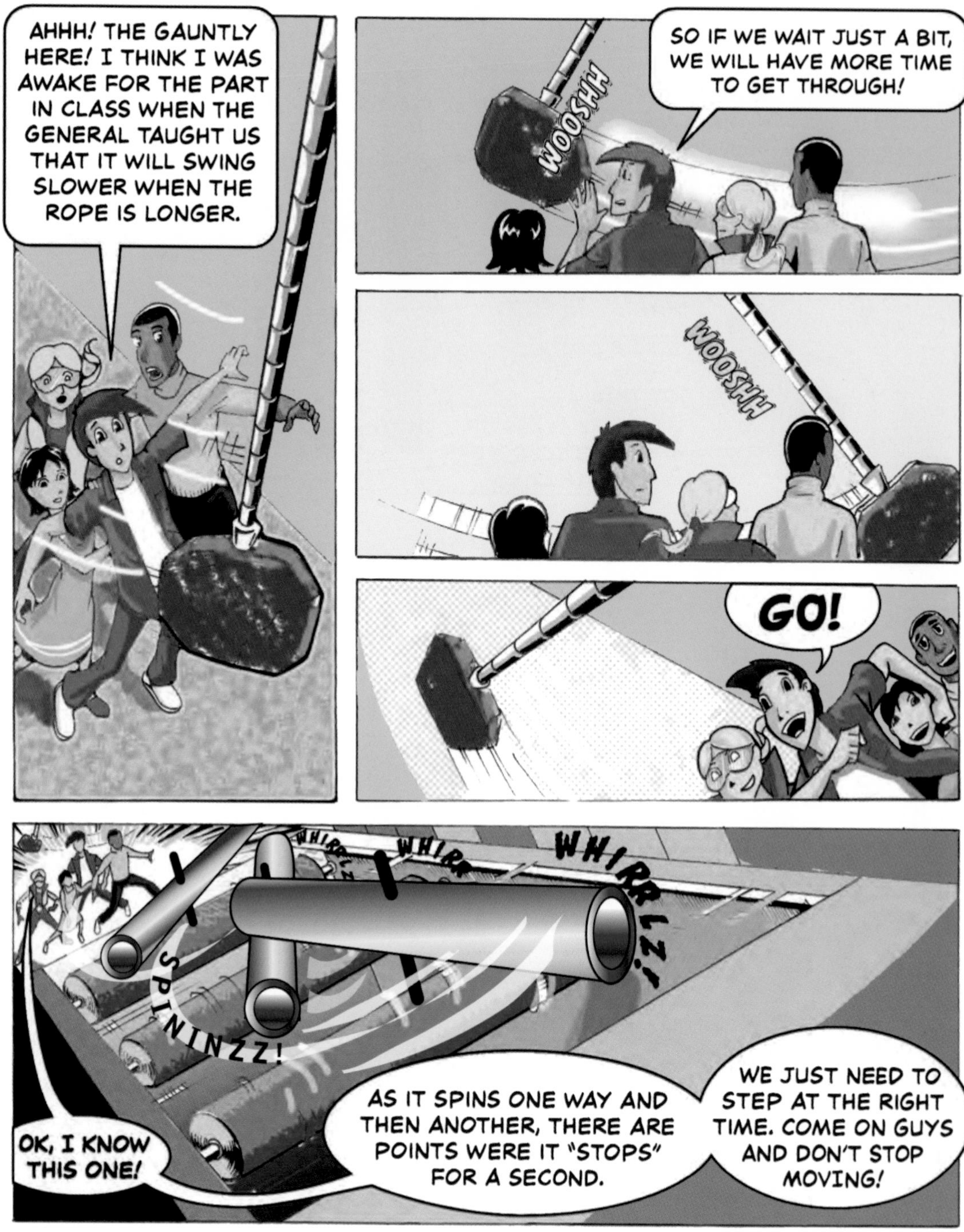
AHHH! THE GAUNTLY HERE! I THINK I WAS AWAKE FOR THE PART IN CLASS WHEN THE GENERAL TAUGHT US THAT IT WILL SWING SLOWER WHEN THE ROPE IS LONGER.
SO IF WE WAIT JUST A BIT, WE WILL HAVE MORE TIME TO GET THROUGH!
WOOSHH
WOOSHH
GO!
WHIRR
WHIRRLZ!!
SPININZZ!
OK, I KNOW THIS ONE!
AS IT SPINS ONE WAY AND THEN ANOTHER, THERE ARE POINTS WERE IT "STOPS" FOR A SECOND.
WE JUST NEED TO STEP AT THE RIGHT TIME. COME ON GUYS AND DON'T STOP MOVING!

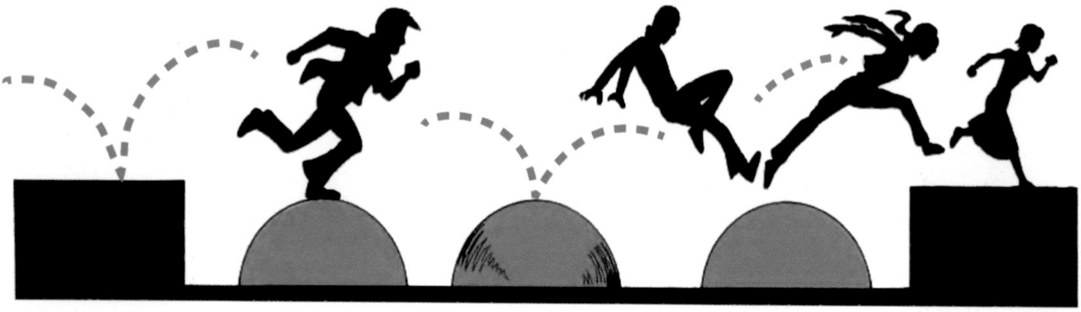

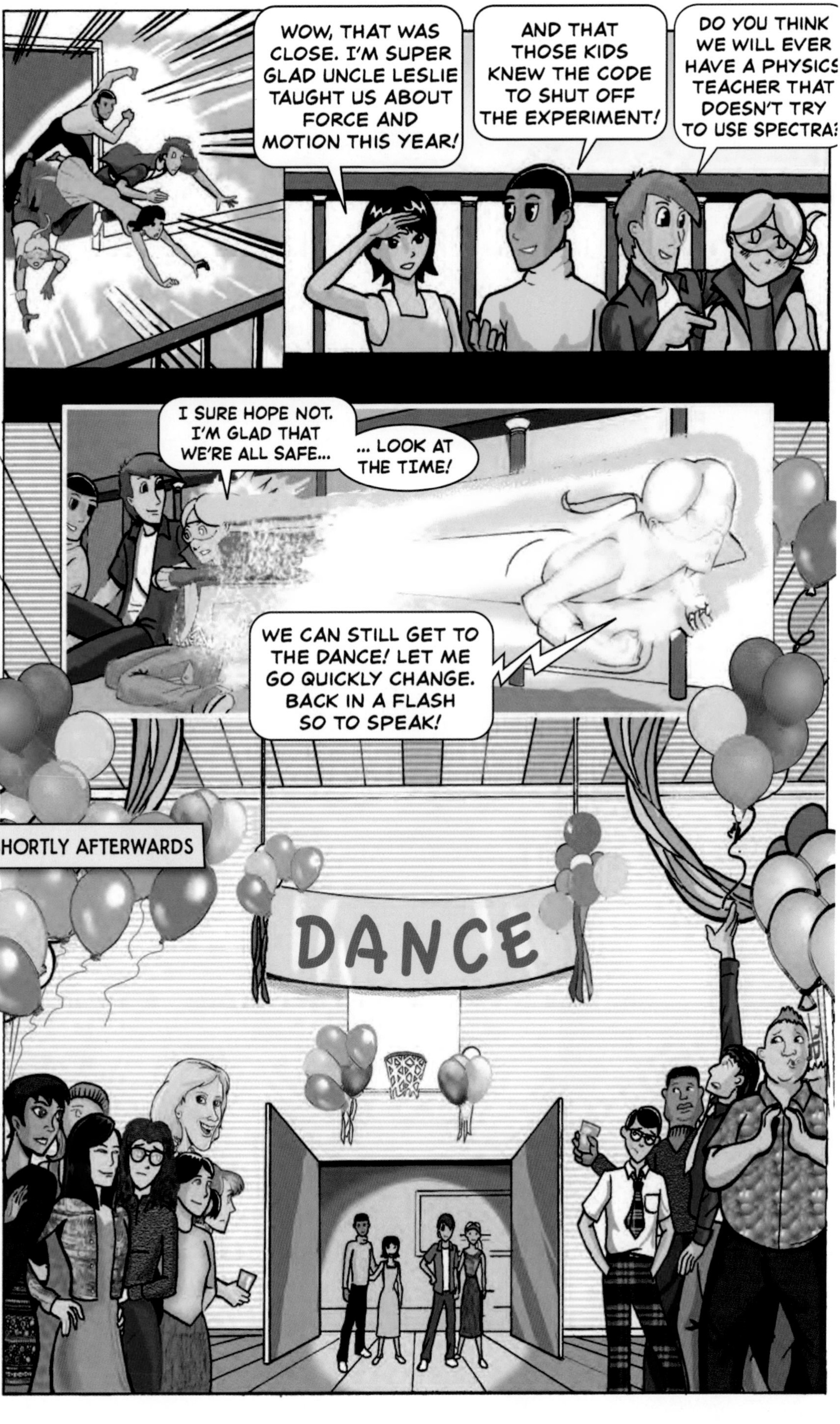
WOW, THAT WAS CLOSE. I'M SUPER GLAD UNCLE LESLIE TAUGHT US ABOUT FORCE AND MOTION THIS YEAR!
AND THAT THOSE KIDS KNEW THE CODE TO SHUT OFF THE EXPERIMENT!
DO YOU THINK WE WILL EVER HAVE A PHYSICS TEACHER THAT DOESN'T TRY TO USE SPECTRA?
I SURE HOPE NOT. I'M GLAD THAT WE'RE ALL SAFE...
... LOOK AT THE TIME!
WE CAN STILL GET TO THE DANCE! LET ME GO QUICKLY CHANGE. BACK IN A FLASH SO TO SPEAK!
SHORTLY AFTERWARDS
DANCE

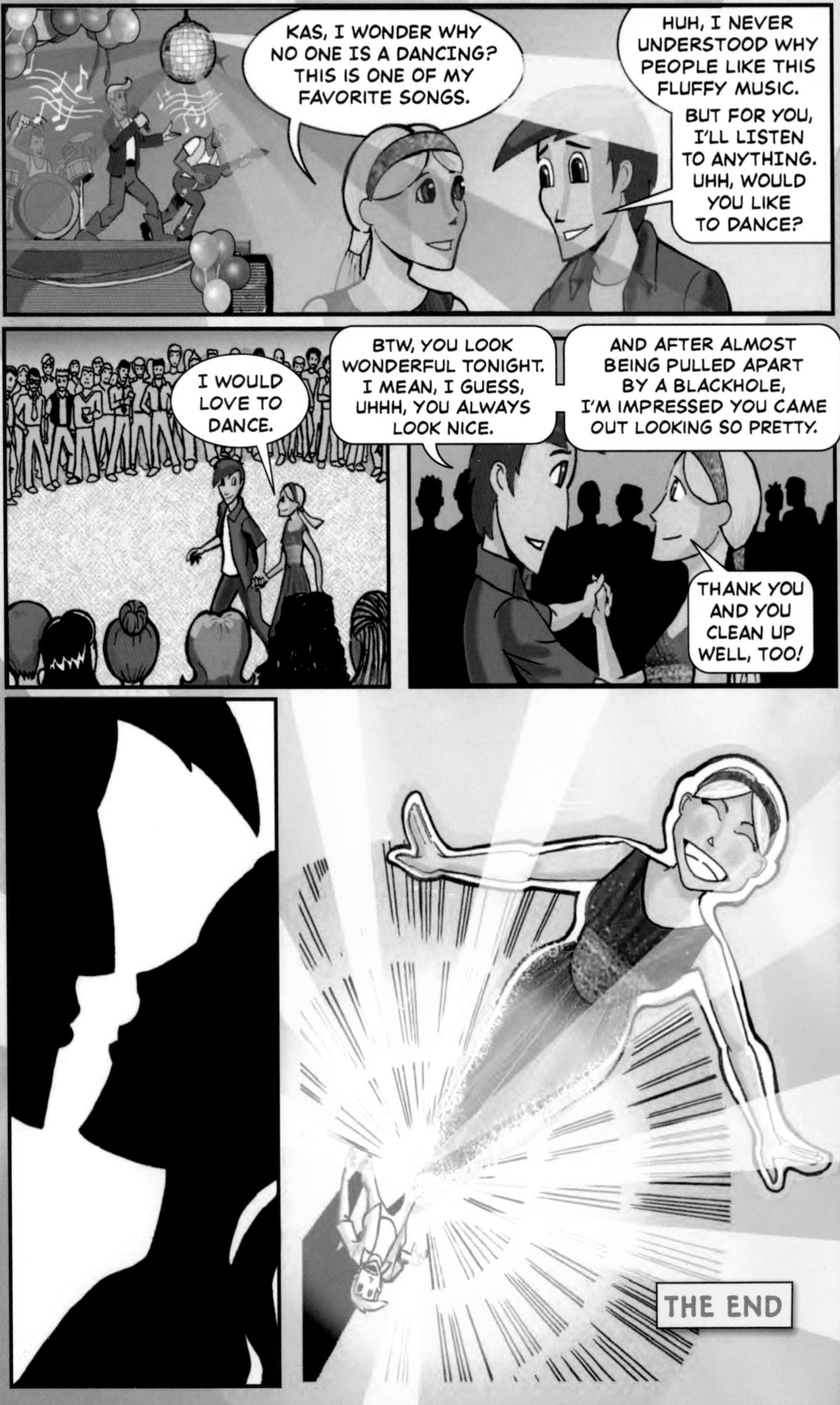
KAS, I WONDER WHY NO ONE IS A DANCING? THIS IS ONE OF MY FAVORITE SONGS.
HUH, I NEVER UNDERSTOOD WHY PEOPLE LIKE THIS FLUFFY MUSIC.
BUT FOR YOU, I'LL LISTEN TO ANYTHING. UHH, WOULD YOU LIKE TO DANCE?
I WOULD LOVE TO DANCE.
BTW, YOU LOOK WONDERFUL TONIGHT. I MEAN, I GUESS, UHHH, YOU ALWAYS LOOK NICE.
AND AFTER ALMOST BEING PULLED APART BY A BLACKHOLE, I'M IMPRESSED YOU CAME OUT LOOKING SO PRETTY.
THANK YOU AND YOU CLEAN UP WELL, TOO!
THE END

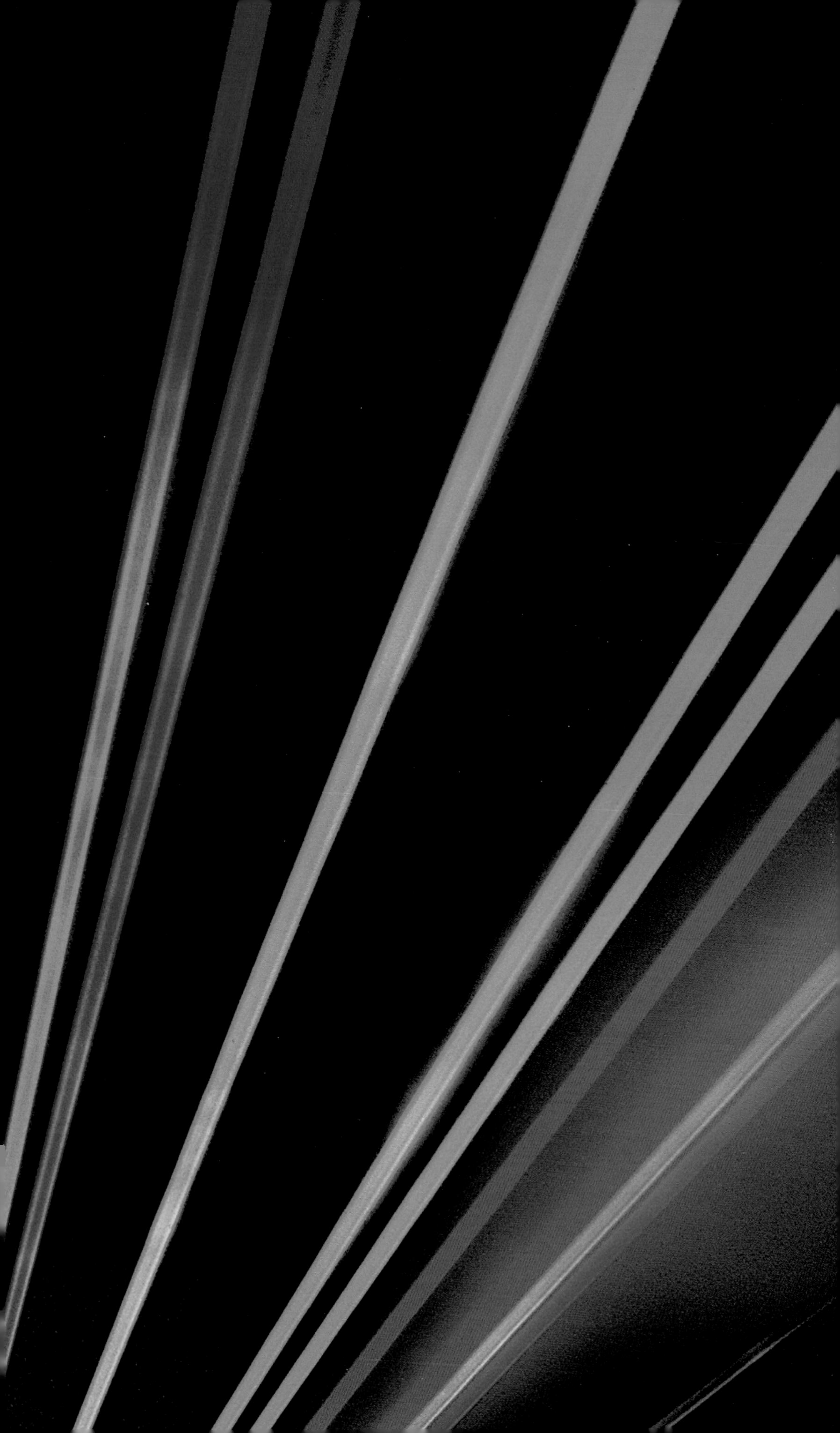

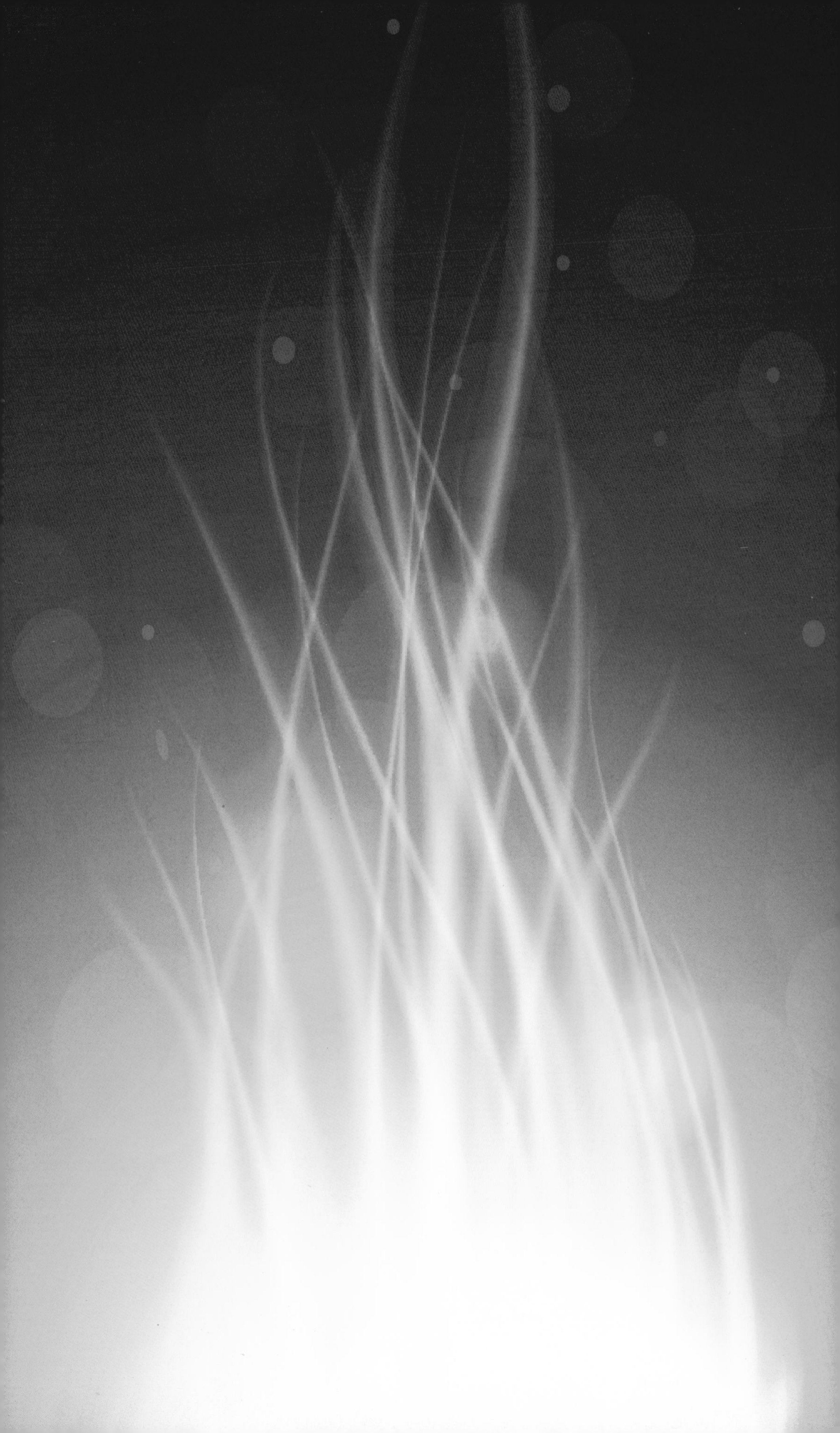

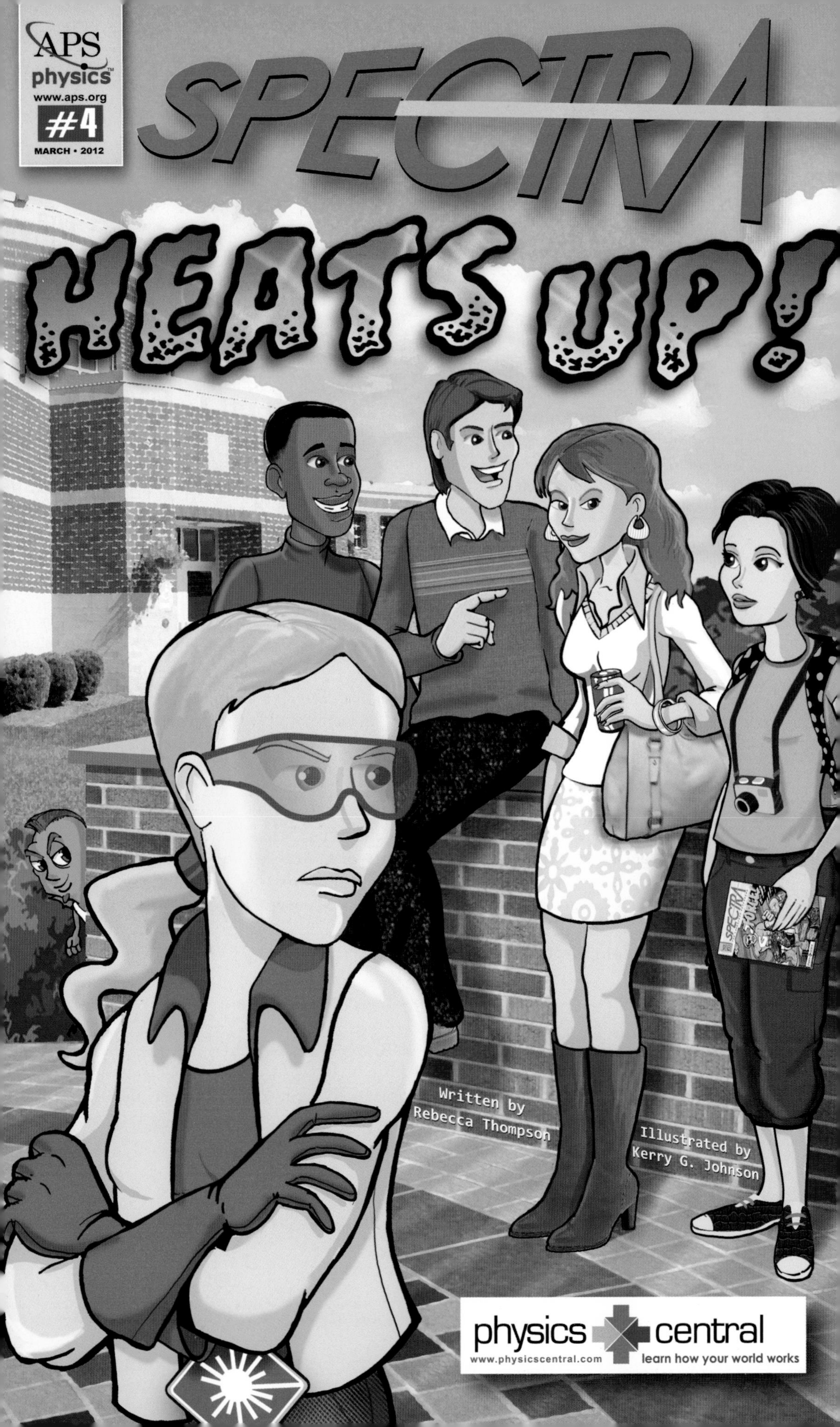
APS
physics™
www.aps.org
#4
MARCH • 2012
SPECTRA
HEATS UP!
Written by
Rebecca Thompson
Illustrated by
Kerry G. Johnson
physics central
www.physicscentral.com
learn how your world works

A note about Maxwell's Demon

James Clerk Maxwell was one of the world's most accomplished physicists. He is best known for his research into electricity and magnetism. If you participated in *PhysicsQuest: Nikola Tesla and the Electric Fair* you may have learned about some of the things he studied. Though many physicists will always associate him with the famed "Maxwell's Equations" which describe how electricity and magnetism behave together and how they make up light, he also studied how groups of particles move together.

The "demon" in this story is based on a thought experiment that Maxwell came up with to discuss how one might get around the natural laws of the universe. As you will learn in both the comic and the PhysicsQuest activities, things in contact with each other like to be the same temperature. This is called "thermal equilibrium." Thermal means heat and equilibrium means the same, the heat is the same in the whole system. You will never have a room where all the cold particles are on one side and all the hot particles are on the other. Or where all the air particles decide they want to go up to one corner of the room. But when Maxwell started thinking about all of this, he thought to himself "Huh, what if there was a little demon that could control where the particles go and what they do?"

He first thought about what would happen to a room if there were a divider and the demon could open and close a door to keep the hot particles on one side and the cold ones on the other. Then he thought about what would happen if the demon let particles go through the door one way but not the other. How was the demon violating the laws of nature? If it took no effort for him to do this, why didn't this just happen in real life? Thinking about this seems a weird way to do science, but such "thought experiments" often help scientists have a better understanding of what is going on in the system. Sometimes when you step back from a complicated problem, and there isn't much more complicated that looking at hundreds of billions of particles at once, you can get a better understanding of how it all works.

This comic takes the idea of "Maxwell's Demon" and brings it to life. Only this time instead of being a thought experiment by the famous James Clerk Maxwell, the demon is an imp controlled by the mean Tiffany Maxwell. He does all the things that he is supposed to do, only this time it doesn't just teach physics, it could cost Spectra's friends their lives.

Some good websites on Maxwell's Demon:

http://www.imsc.res.in/~sitabhra/research/persistence/maxwell.html

http://www.auburn.edu/~smith01/notes/maxdem.htm

http://splasho.com/blog/essays/maxwell-thermodynamics-meets-the-demon/

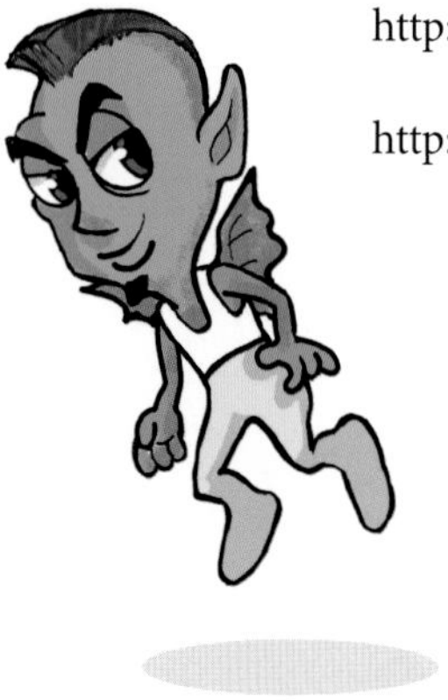

PUBLISHED BY THE AMERICAN PHYSICAL SOCIETY © 2012

SPECTRA HEATS UP!

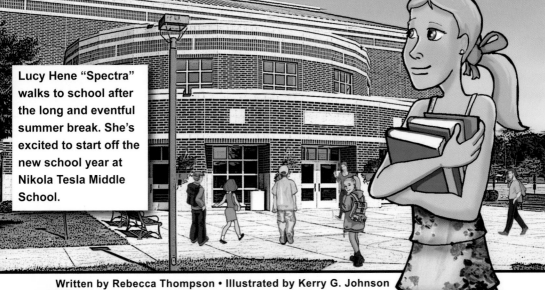

Lucy Hene "Spectra" walks to school after the long and eventful summer break. She's excited to start off the new school year at Nikola Tesla Middle School.

Written by Rebecca Thompson • Illustrated by Kerry G. Johnson

HEY!!

HUH, I THOUGHT THIS WAS A MIDDLE SCHOOL, I DIDN'T KNOW THEY WERE LETTING 5TH GRADERS IN HERE.

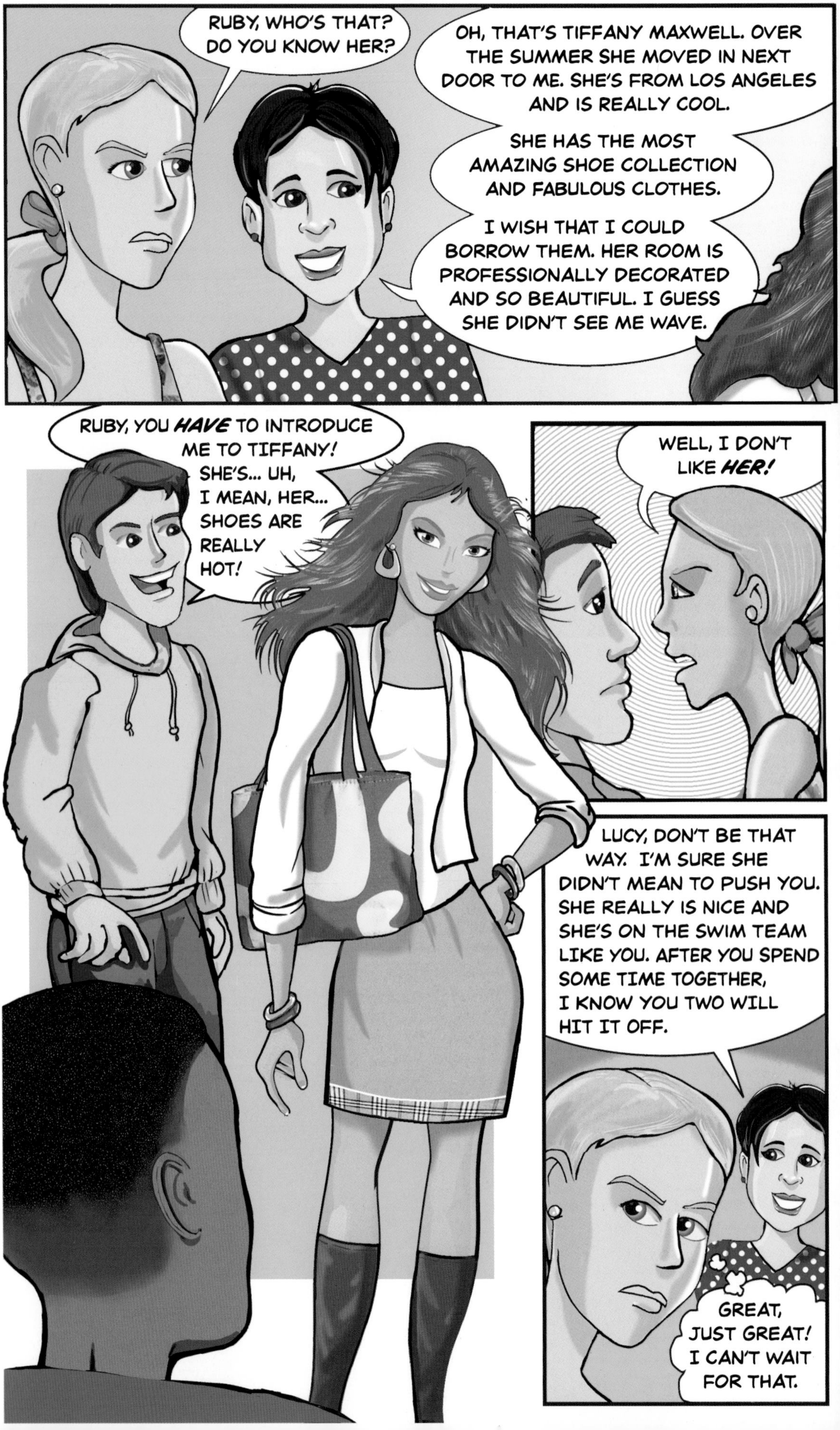
RUBY, WHO'S THAT? DO YOU KNOW HER?
OH, THAT'S TIFFANY MAXWELL. OVER THE SUMMER SHE MOVED IN NEXT DOOR TO ME. SHE'S FROM LOS ANGELES AND IS REALLY COOL.
SHE HAS THE MOST AMAZING SHOE COLLECTION AND FABULOUS CLOTHES.
I WISH THAT I COULD BORROW THEM. HER ROOM IS PROFESSIONALLY DECORATED AND SO BEAUTIFUL. I GUESS SHE DIDN'T SEE ME WAVE.
RUBY, YOU ***HAVE*** TO INTRODUCE ME TO TIFFANY! SHE'S... UH, I MEAN, HER... SHOES ARE REALLY HOT!
WELL, I DON'T LIKE ***HER!***
LUCY, DON'T BE THAT WAY. I'M SURE SHE DIDN'T MEAN TO PUSH YOU. SHE REALLY IS NICE AND SHE'S ON THE SWIM TEAM LIKE YOU. AFTER YOU SPEND SOME TIME TOGETHER, I KNOW YOU TWO WILL HIT IT OFF.
GREAT, JUST GREAT! I CAN'T WAIT FOR THAT.

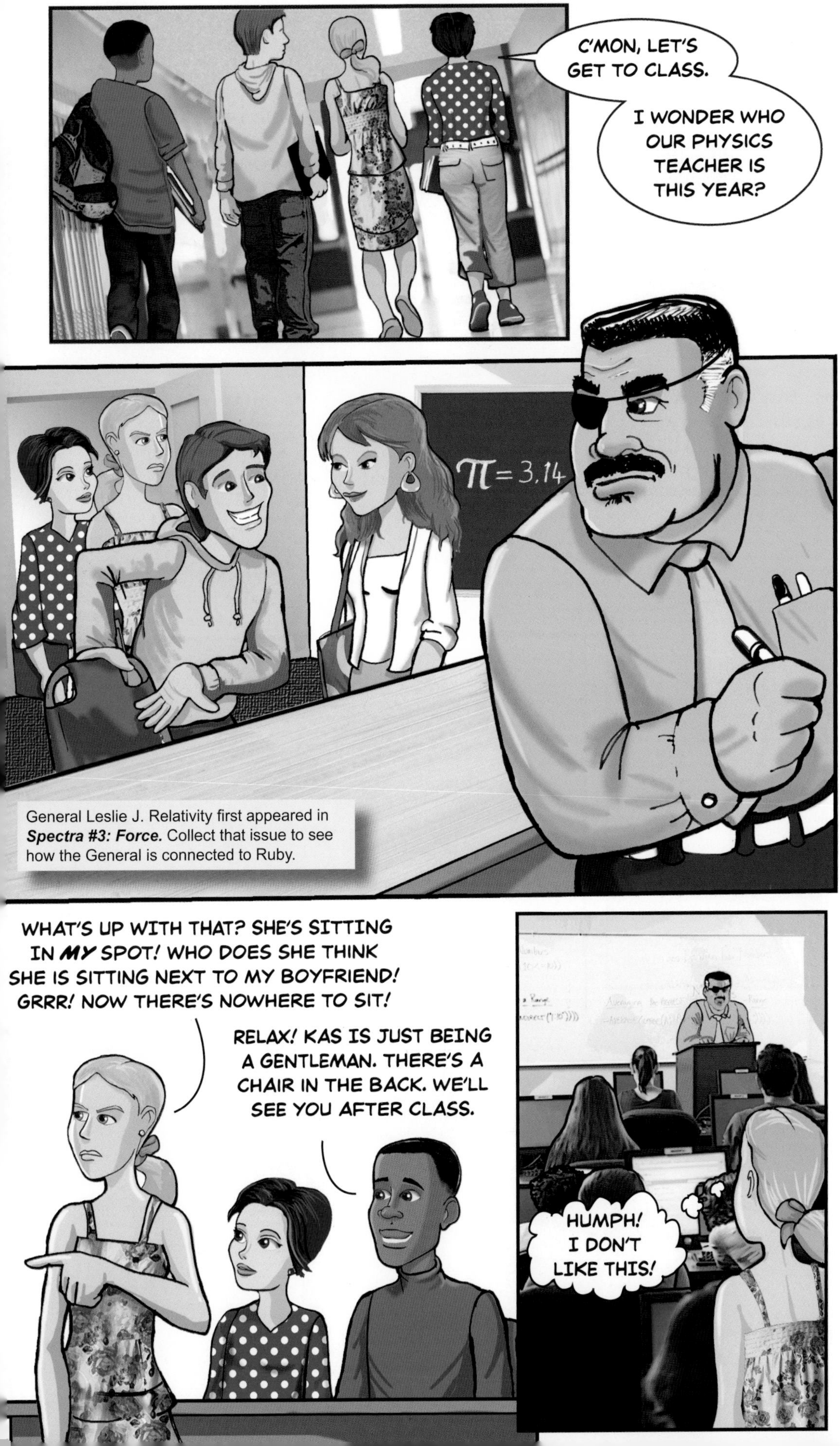
C'MON, LET'S GET TO CLASS.
I WONDER WHO OUR PHYSICS TEACHER IS THIS YEAR?
π = 3.14
General Leslie J. Relativity first appeared in ***Spectra #3: Force.*** Collect that issue to see how the General is connected to Ruby.
WHAT'S UP WITH THAT? SHE'S SITTING IN ***MY*** SPOT! WHO DOES SHE THINK SHE IS SITTING NEXT TO MY BOYFRIEND! GRRR! NOW THERE'S NOWHERE TO SIT!
RELAX! KAS IS JUST BEING A GENTLEMAN. THERE'S A CHAIR IN THE BACK. WE'LL SEE YOU AFTER CLASS.
HUMPH! I DON'T LIKE THIS!

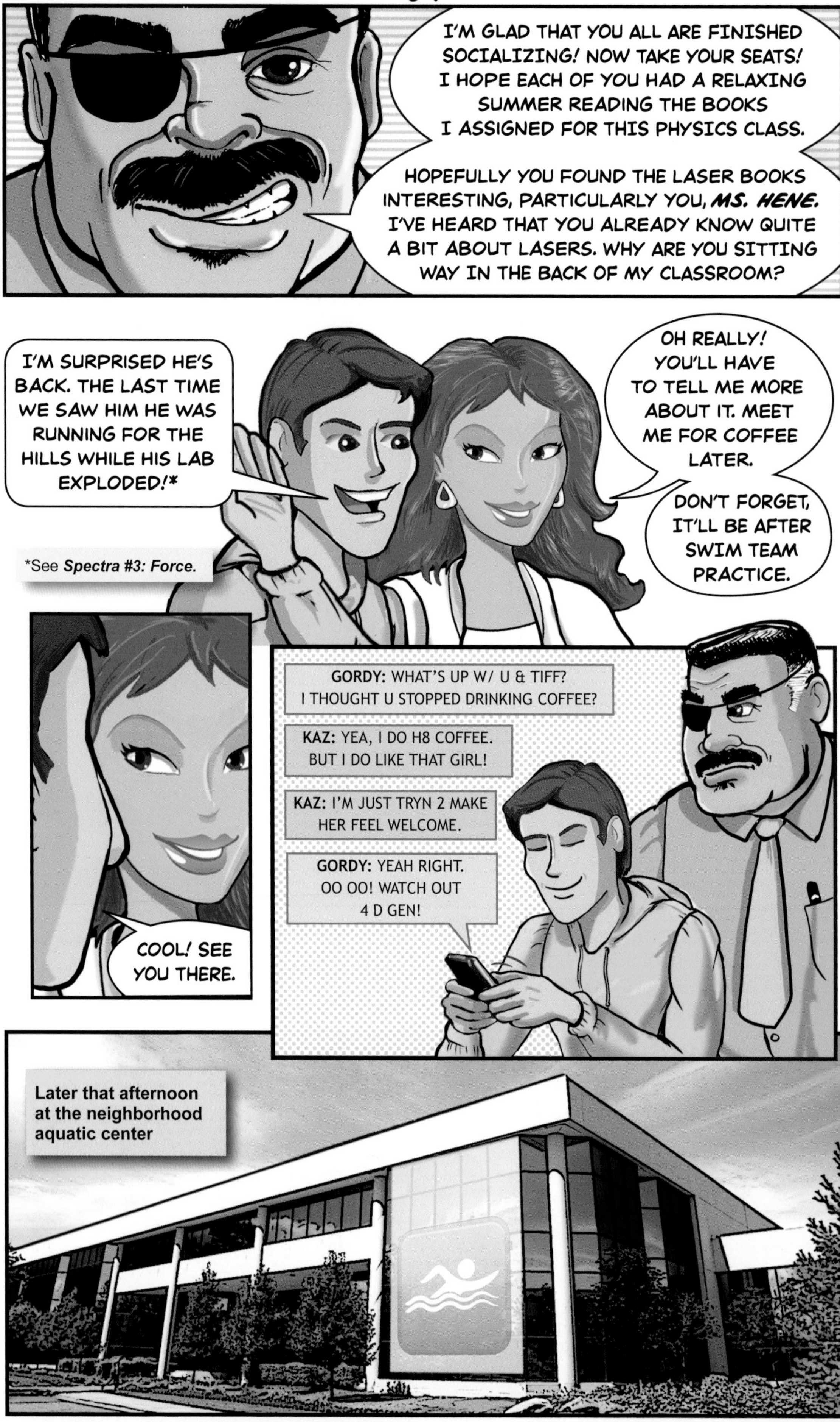
I'M GLAD THAT YOU ALL ARE FINISHED SOCIALIZING! NOW TAKE YOUR SEATS! I HOPE EACH OF YOU HAD A RELAXING SUMMER READING THE BOOKS I ASSIGNED FOR THIS PHYSICS CLASS.
HOPEFULLY YOU FOUND THE LASER BOOKS INTERESTING, PARTICULARLY YOU, MS. HENE. I'VE HEARD THAT YOU ALREADY KNOW QUITE A BIT ABOUT LASERS. WHY ARE YOU SITTING WAY IN THE BACK OF MY CLASSROOM?
I'M SURPRISED HE'S BACK. THE LAST TIME WE SAW HIM HE WAS RUNNING FOR THE HILLS WHILE HIS LAB EXPLODED!*
OH REALLY! YOU'LL HAVE TO TELL ME MORE ABOUT IT. MEET ME FOR COFFEE LATER.
DON'T FORGET, IT'LL BE AFTER SWIM TEAM PRACTICE.
*See Spectra #3: Force.
COOL! SEE YOU THERE.
GORDY: WHAT'S UP W/ U & TIFF? I THOUGHT U STOPPED DRINKING COFFEE?
KAZ: YEA, I DO H8 COFFEE. BUT I DO LIKE THAT GIRL!
KAZ: I'M JUST TRYN 2 MAKE HER FEEL WELCOME.
GORDY: YEAH RIGHT. OO OO! WATCH OUT 4 D GEN!
Later that afternoon at the neighborhood aquatic center

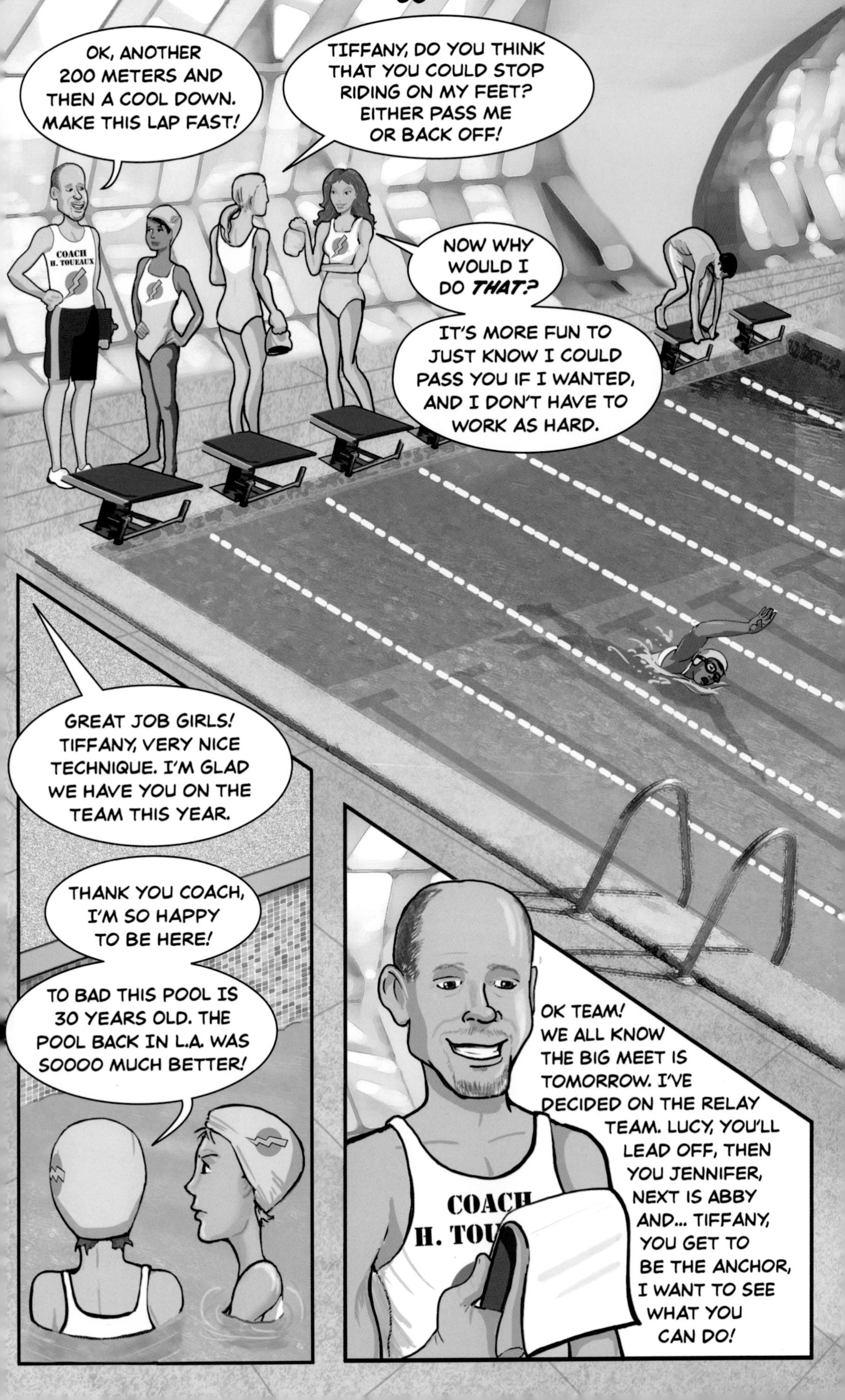
OK, ANOTHER 200 METERS AND THEN A COOL DOWN. MAKE THIS LAP FAST!
TIFFANY, DO YOU THINK THAT YOU COULD STOP RIDING ON MY FEET? EITHER PASS ME OR BACK OFF!
COACH H. TOUEAUX
NOW WHY WOULD I DO *THAT?*
IT'S MORE FUN TO JUST KNOW I COULD PASS YOU IF I WANTED, AND I DON'T HAVE TO WORK AS HARD.
GREAT JOB GIRLS! TIFFANY, VERY NICE TECHNIQUE. I'M GLAD WE HAVE YOU ON THE TEAM THIS YEAR.
THANK YOU COACH, I'M SO HAPPY TO BE HERE!
TO BAD THIS POOL IS 30 YEARS OLD. THE POOL BACK IN L.A. WAS SOOOO MUCH BETTER!
OK TEAM! WE ALL KNOW THE BIG MEET IS TOMORROW. I'VE DECIDED ON THE RELAY TEAM. LUCY, YOU'LL LEAD OFF, THEN YOU JENNIFER, NEXT IS ABBY AND... TIFFANY, YOU GET TO BE THE ANCHOR, I WANT TO SEE WHAT YOU CAN DO!
COACH H. TOU

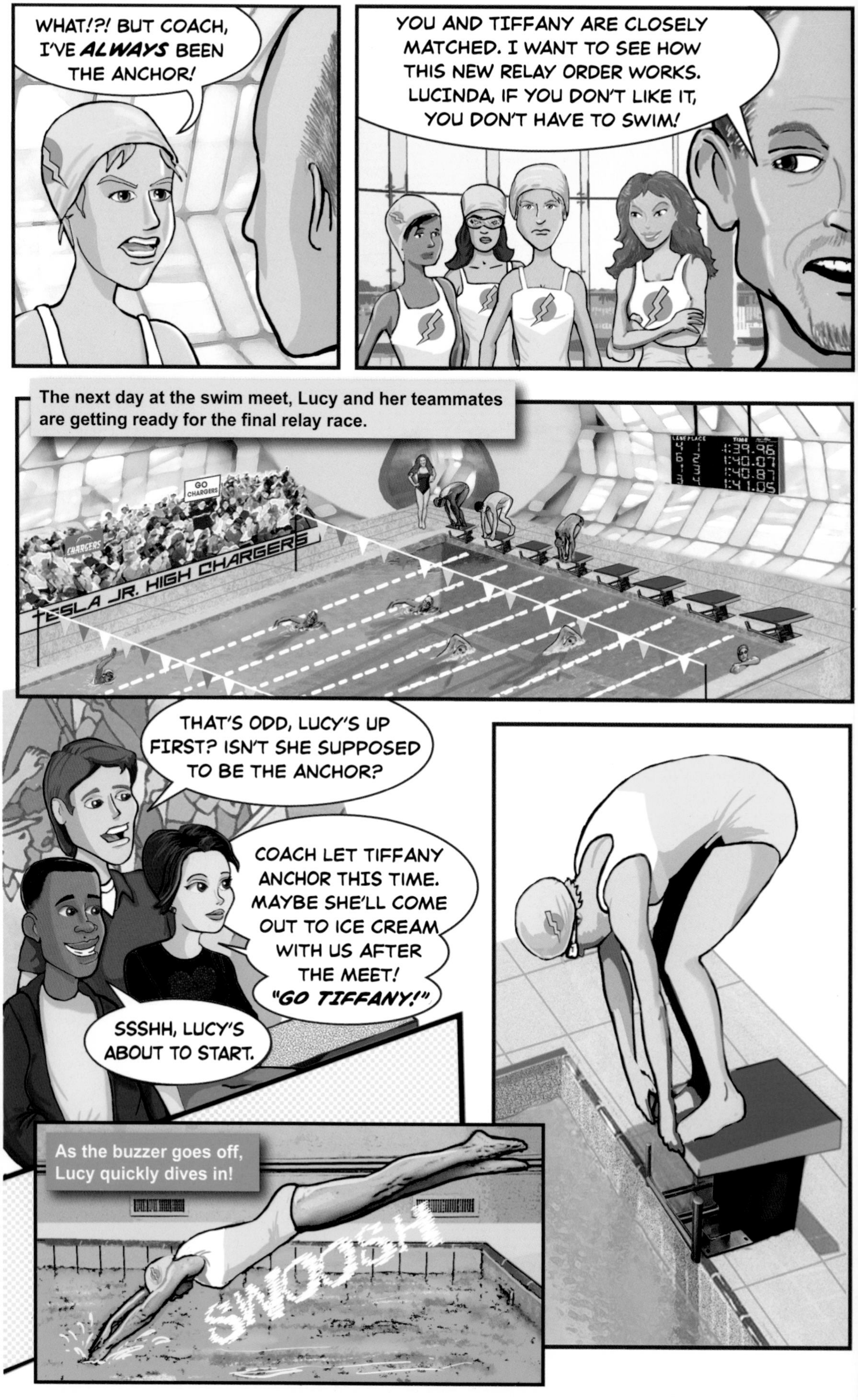
WHAT!?! BUT COACH, I'VE ALWAYS BEEN THE ANCHOR!
YOU AND TIFFANY ARE CLOSELY MATCHED. I WANT TO SEE HOW THIS NEW RELAY ORDER WORKS. LUCINDA, IF YOU DON'T LIKE IT, YOU DON'T HAVE TO SWIM!
The next day at the swim meet, Lucy and her teammates are getting ready for the final relay race.
GO CHARGERS
CHARGERS
TESLA JR. HIGH CHARGERS
THAT'S ODD, LUCY'S UP FIRST? ISN'T SHE SUPPOSED TO BE THE ANCHOR?
COACH LET TIFFANY ANCHOR THIS TIME. MAYBE SHE'LL COME OUT TO ICE CREAM WITH US AFTER THE MEET! "GO TIFFANY!"
SSSHH, LUCY'S ABOUT TO START.
As the buzzer goes off, Lucy quickly dives in!
SWOOSH

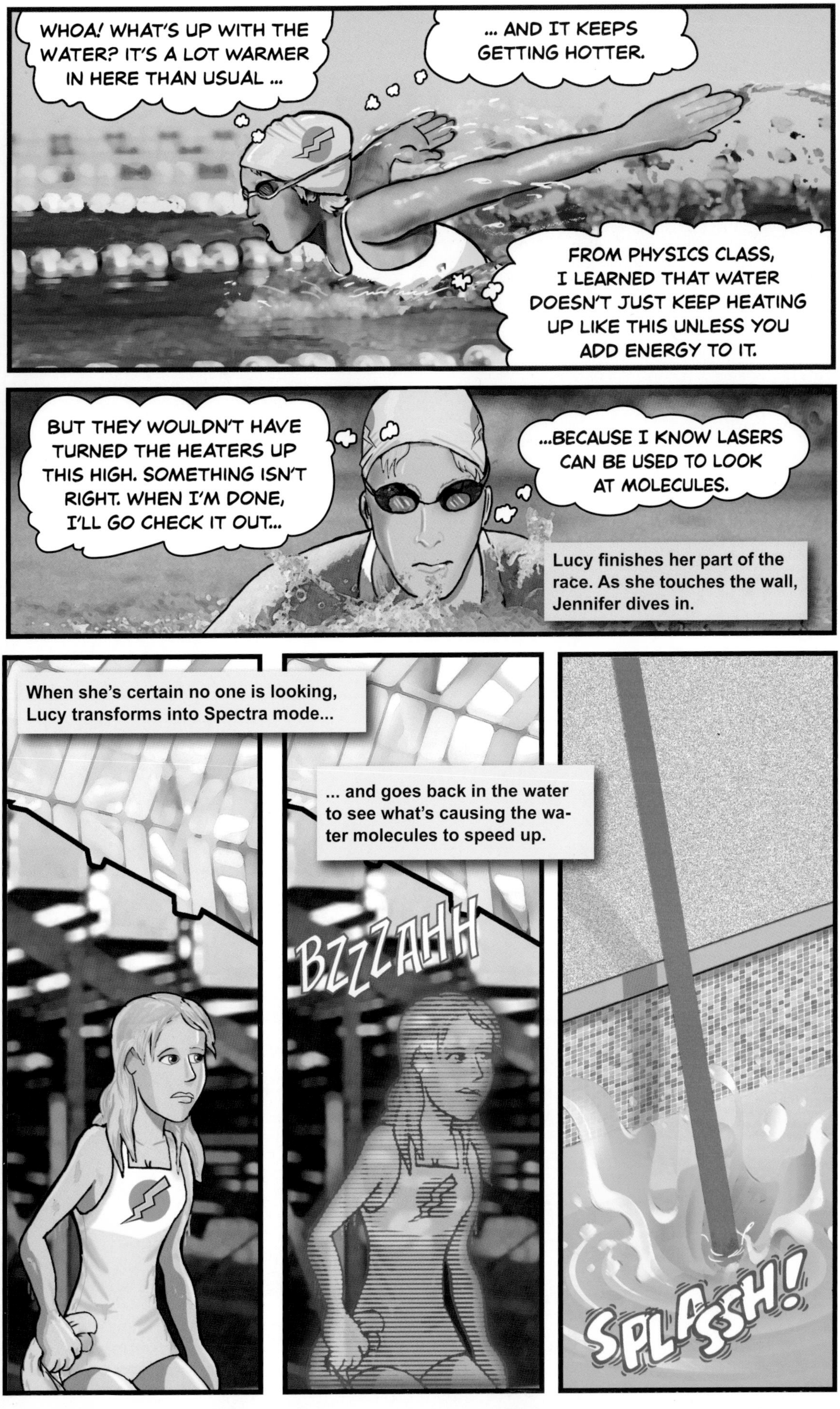
WHOA! WHAT'S UP WITH THE WATER? IT'S A LOT WARMER IN HERE THAN USUAL ...
... AND IT KEEPS GETTING HOTTER.
FROM PHYSICS CLASS, I LEARNED THAT WATER DOESN'T JUST KEEP HEATING UP LIKE THIS UNLESS YOU ADD ENERGY TO IT.
BUT THEY WOULDN'T HAVE TURNED THE HEATERS UP THIS HIGH. SOMETHING ISN'T RIGHT. WHEN I'M DONE, I'LL GO CHECK IT OUT...
...BECAUSE I KNOW LASERS CAN BE USED TO LOOK AT MOLECULES.
Lucy finishes her part of the race. As she touches the wall, Jennifer dives in.
When she's certain no one is looking, Lucy transforms into Spectra mode...
... and goes back in the water to see what's causing the water molecules to speed up.
BZZZAHH
SPLASSH!

As she swims in her Spectra "laser" form, she spots an object speeding across the pool.

WHAT'S THAT? IS IT A TOY? IT'S MOVING VERY FAST AND IT'S HITTING THE WATER MOLECULES TO MAKE THEM GO FASTER. I BET THAT'S THE CAUSE OF THIS OVERHEATED POOL!

I SHOULD CATCH IT BEFORE SOMEONE GETS HURT.

WOW! IT'S MOVING TOO FAST! I CAN'T REACH IT!

ZOOM!

Spectra exerted all her strength trying to catch the object. She needs to take a break so she heads back up to the deck.

WHAT'S GOING ON AND WHY IS TIFFANY SO RED AND SPLOTCHY?

I DON'T KNOW WHAT HAPPENED... IT JUST GOT REALLY HOT!

I JUST COULDN'T FINISH THE RACE!

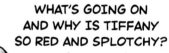

OH TIFFANY! ARE YOU ALRIGHT? WE SAW EVERY-THING. I'M SO SORRY! WHAT CAN I DO TO HELP?

RUBY, DON'T *TOUCH* ME! I DON'T NEED YOUR HELP!

An agitated Tiffany stomps off to the locker room.

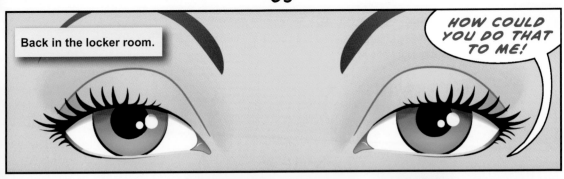

HOW COULD YOU DO THAT TO ME!

Back in the locker room.

YOU WERE JUST SUPPOSED TO HEAT UP THE OTHER TEAM SO OUR RELAY COULD WIN AND I WOULD LOOK LIKE A HERO!

INSTEAD YOU... WAIT, SHH... BE QUIET! DO YOU HEAR THAT?

HOW COULD YOU DO THAT TO TIFFANY?

I KNOW YOU'RE JEALOUS BUT THAT JUST WASN'T RIGHT!

WHAT ARE YOU TALKING ABOUT? I ADMIT THE POOL GETTING HOT WAS CRAZY, BUT THAT WASN'T CAUSED BY ME!

YEAH, RIGHT. I DIDN'T SEE YOU WHEN THE POOL GOT HOT! THE GUYS AND I THOUGHT SPECTRA CAUSED THE CHAOS.

IN UNCLE LESLIE'S PHYSICS CLASS WE LEARNED THAT LASERS ARE USED TO MAKE THINGS VERY HOT.

LASERS USE THEIR ENERGY TO PUSH MOLECULES AROUND AND HEAT THEM UP.

I DON'T KNOW OF ANYONE ELSE IN THE POOL THAT COULD HAVE DONE THAT!

A BIT OF A COINCIDENCE, DON'T YOU THINK?

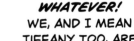

I DON'T KNOW WHAT'S HAPPENING. SO *SPECTRA* WENT TO INVESTIGATE. THAT'S WHY I WAS MISSING. BLAMING ME JUST ISN'T FAIR!

WHATEVER! WE, AND I MEAN TIFFANY TOO, ARE ALL GOING OUT FOR ICE CREAM. JOIN US IF YOU'RE WILLING TO APOLOGIZE TO *HER!*

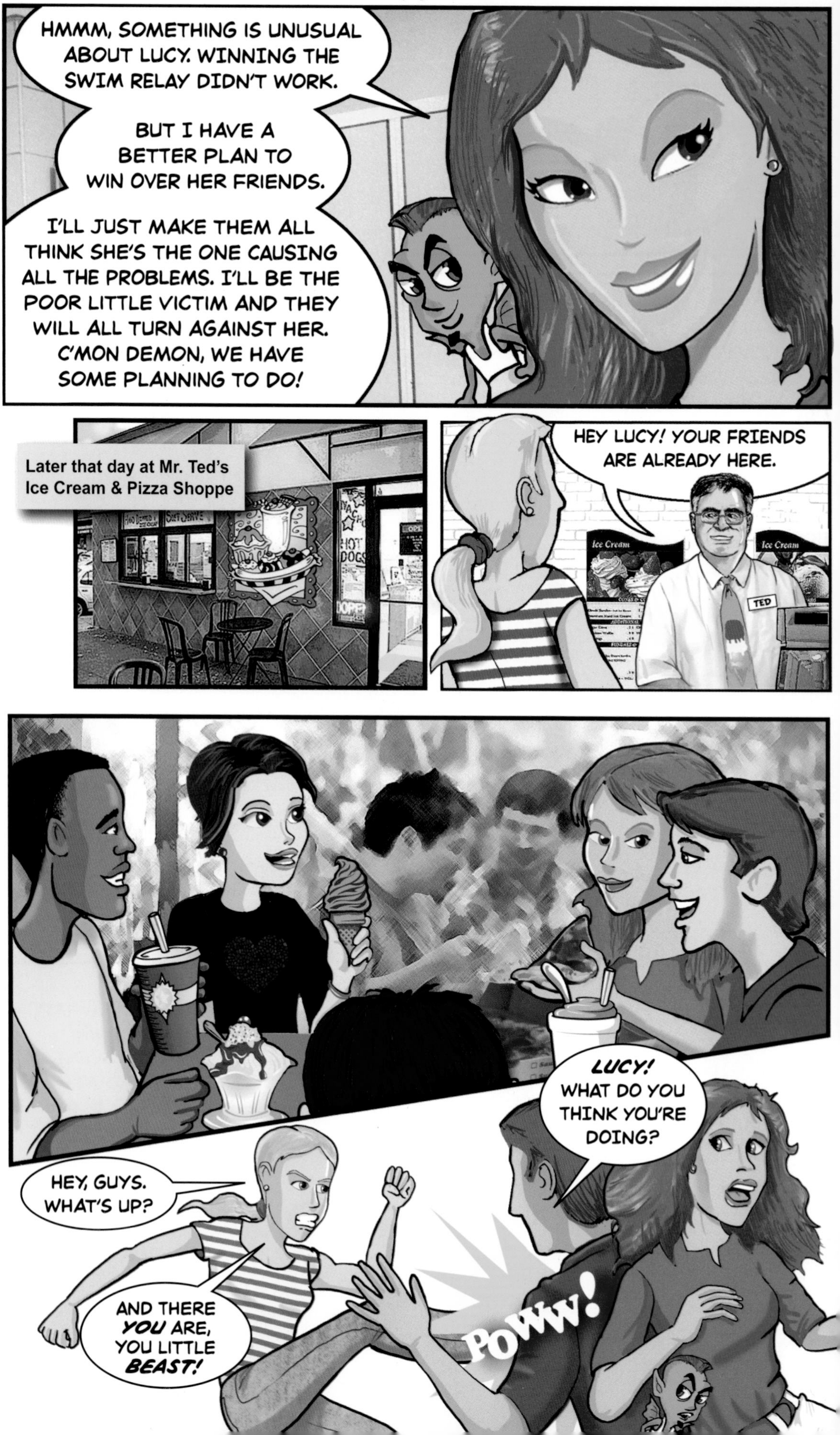
HMMM, SOMETHING IS UNUSUAL ABOUT LUCY. WINNING THE SWIM RELAY DIDN'T WORK.
BUT I HAVE A BETTER PLAN TO WIN OVER HER FRIENDS.
I'LL JUST MAKE THEM ALL THINK SHE'S THE ONE CAUSING ALL THE PROBLEMS. I'LL BE THE POOR LITTLE VICTIM AND THEY WILL ALL TURN AGAINST HER. C'MON DEMON, WE HAVE SOME PLANNING TO DO!
Later that day at Mr. Ted's Ice Cream & Pizza Shoppe
HEY LUCY! YOUR FRIENDS ARE ALREADY HERE.
TED
HEY, GUYS. WHAT'S UP?
AND THERE YOU ARE, YOU LITTLE BEAST!
LUCY! WHAT DO YOU THINK YOU'RE DOING?
POWW!

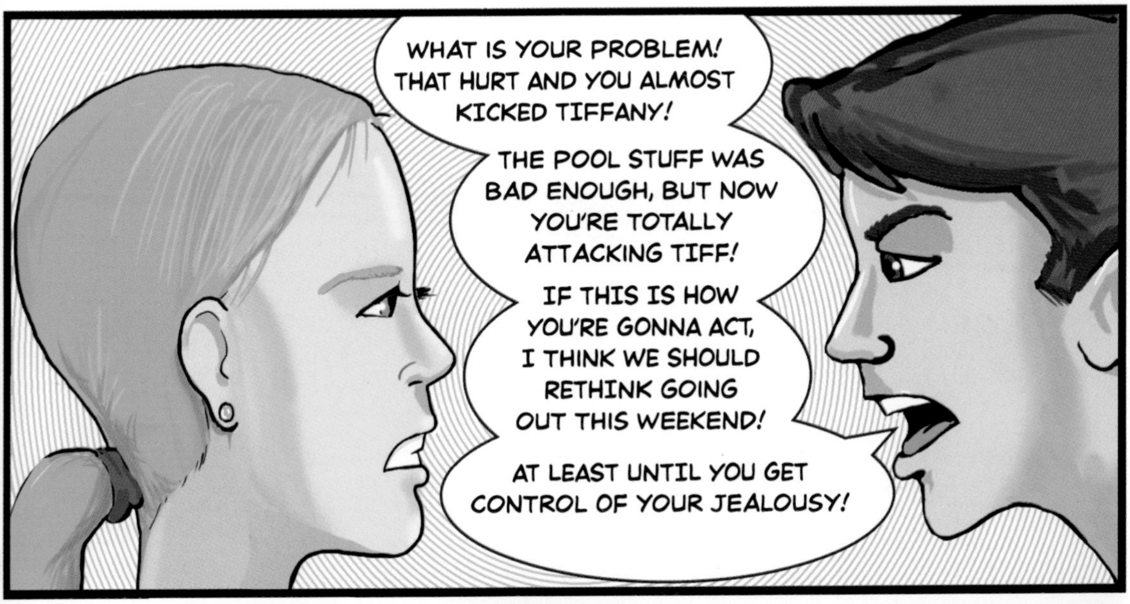
WHAT IS YOUR PROBLEM! THAT HURT AND YOU ALMOST KICKED TIFFANY!
THE POOL STUFF WAS BAD ENOUGH, BUT NOW YOU'RE TOTALLY ATTACKING TIFF!
IF THIS IS HOW YOU'RE GONNA ACT, I THINK WE SHOULD RETHINK GOING OUT THIS WEEKEND!
AT LEAST UNTIL YOU GET CONTROL OF YOUR JEALOUSY!

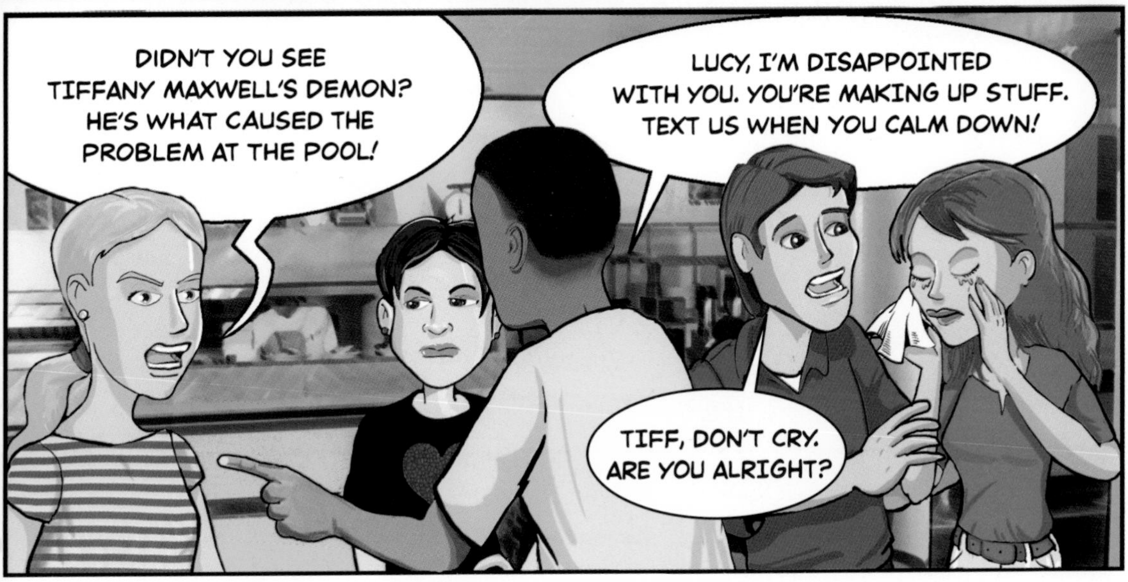
DIDN'T YOU SEE TIFFANY MAXWELL'S DEMON? HE'S WHAT CAUSED THE PROBLEM AT THE POOL!
LUCY, I'M DISAPPOINTED WITH YOU. YOU'RE MAKING UP STUFF. TEXT US WHEN YOU CALM DOWN!
TIFF, DON'T CRY. ARE YOU ALRIGHT?

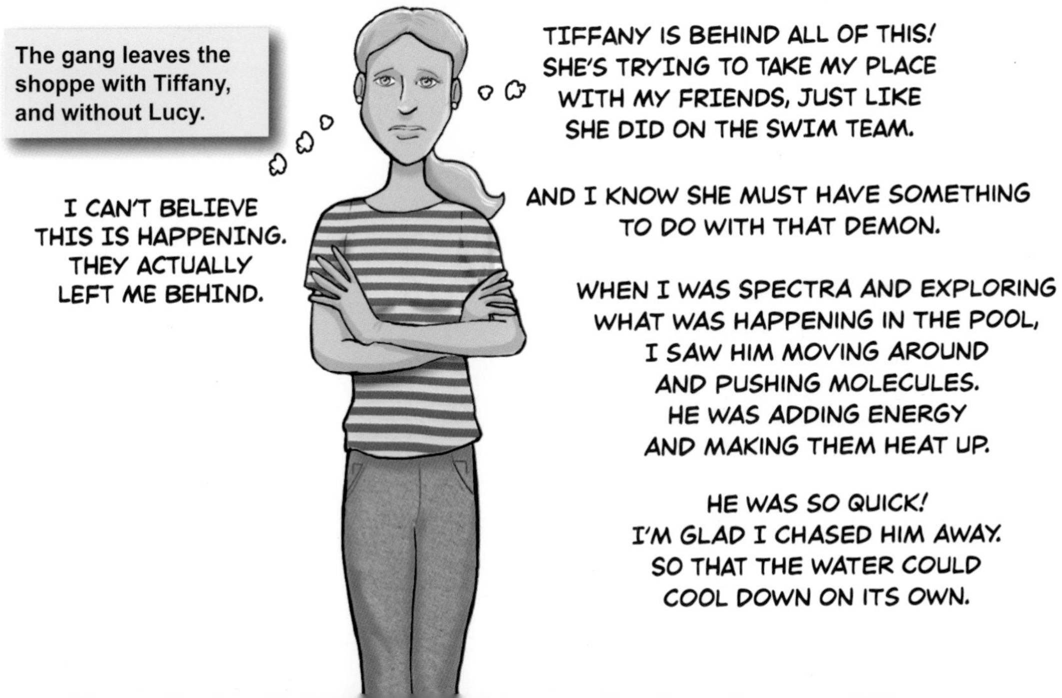
The gang leaves the shoppe with Tiffany, and without Lucy.
I CAN'T BELIEVE THIS IS HAPPENING. THEY ACTUALLY LEFT ME BEHIND.
TIFFANY IS BEHIND ALL OF THIS! SHE'S TRYING TO TAKE MY PLACE WITH MY FRIENDS, JUST LIKE SHE DID ON THE SWIM TEAM.
AND I KNOW SHE MUST HAVE SOMETHING TO DO WITH THAT DEMON.
WHEN I WAS SPECTRA AND EXPLORING WHAT WAS HAPPENING IN THE POOL, I SAW HIM MOVING AROUND AND PUSHING MOLECULES. HE WAS ADDING ENERGY AND MAKING THEM HEAT UP.
HE WAS SO QUICK! I'M GLAD I CHASED HIM AWAY. SO THAT THE WATER COULD COOL DOWN ON ITS OWN.

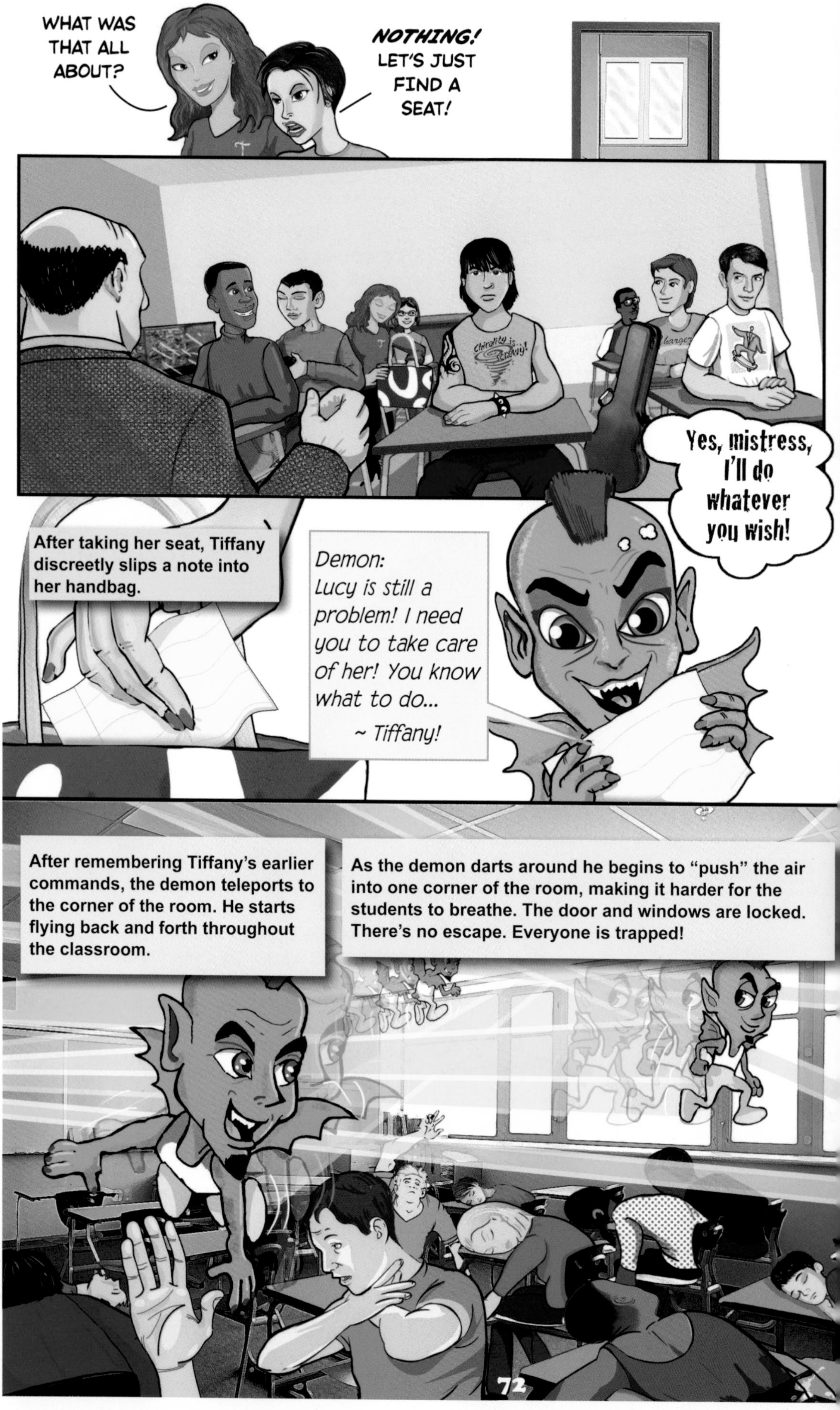
WHAT WAS THAT ALL ABOUT?
NOTHING! LET'S JUST FIND A SEAT!
Chirality is Strong!
Yes, mistress, I'll do whatever you wish!
After taking her seat, Tiffany discreetly slips a note into her handbag.
Demon:
Lucy is still a problem! I need you to take care of her! You know what to do...
~ Tiffany!
After remembering Tiffany's earlier commands, the demon teleports to the corner of the room. He starts flying back and forth throughout the classroom.
As the demon darts around he begins to "push" the air into one corner of the room, making it harder for the students to breathe. The door and windows are locked. There's no escape. Everyone is trapped!

Since Lucy's not in the classroom, she'll get the blame!

I screwed up at the pool. This time I'm gonna make Mistress Tiffany proud! Everyone dies! Sorry Mistress, that you got trapped. I guess you'll die, too.

While resting in her glass tank, Jiggles* the iguana, senses something is wrong with the class. She knows she must get help.

*Jiggles first appeared in *Spectra #2: Power.* Who is Jiggles owner?

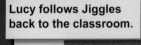
Jiggles finds Lucy in the hallway.

WHAT IS IT JIGGLES AND HOW DID YOU GET OUT OF YOUR TANK?

IS TIMMY STUCK IN THE WELL? WAIT, NO WRONG SHOW, BUT THERE IS SOMETHING WRONG! *SHOW ME!*

Lucy follows Jiggles back to the classroom.

OMG!! THE CLASS NEEDS HELP AND THE DOOR IS LOCKED! IF ONLY I COULD GO THROUGH GLASS!

WHAT AM I TALKING ABOUT? I CAN DO THIS! I HAVE THE POWER OF A *LASER!*

FBUZZZ!

WOW, ITS THE SAME ROOM NUMBER AS OUR LAST TEST ANSWERS. I'M GLAD WE ALL DID WELL ON THE TEST!

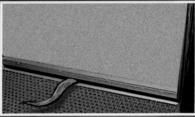

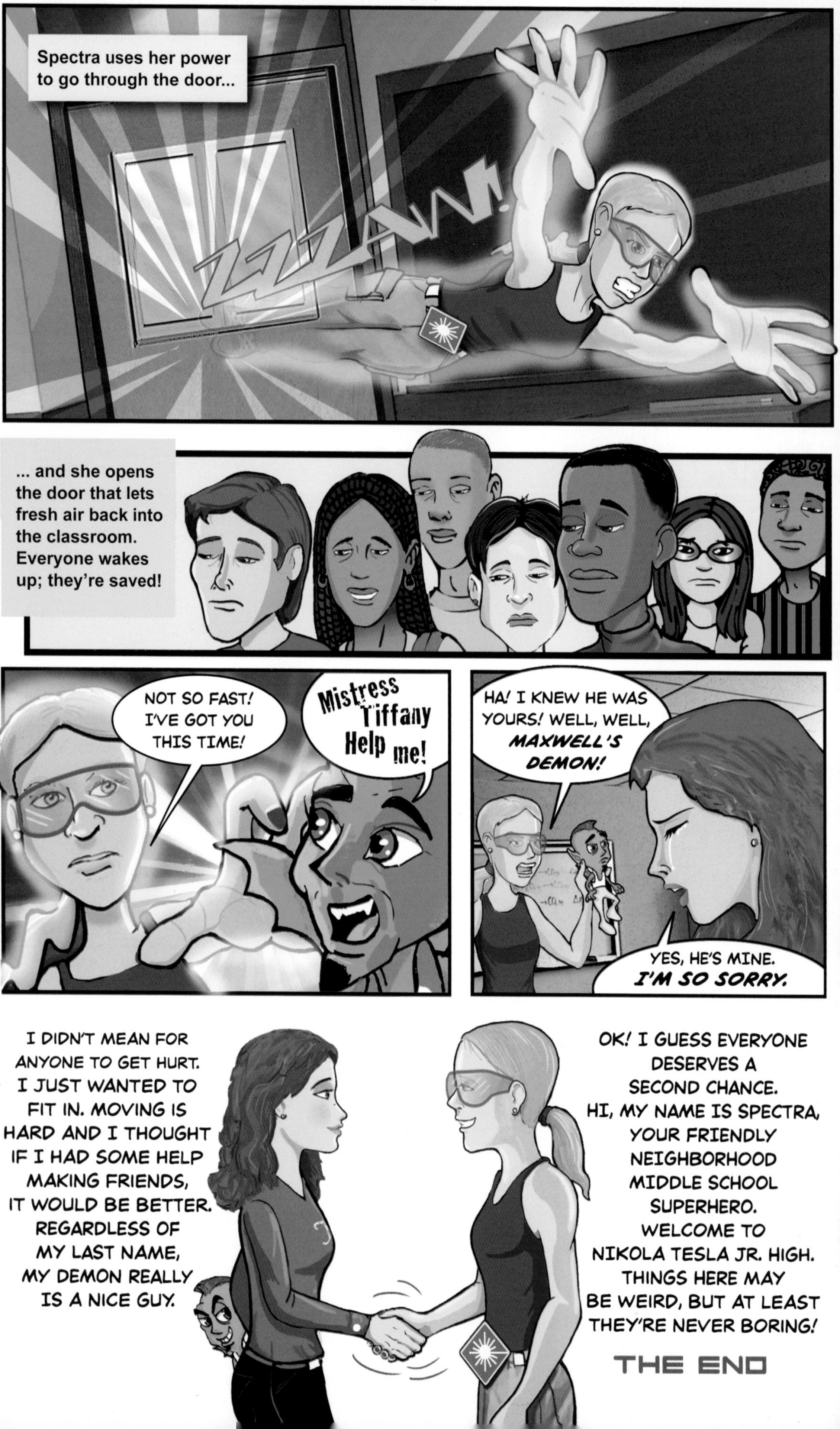
Spectra uses her power to go through the door...
... and she opens the door that lets fresh air back into the classroom. Everyone wakes up; they're saved!
NOT SO FAST! I'VE GOT YOU THIS TIME!
Mistress Tiffany Help me!
HA! I KNEW HE WAS YOURS! WELL, WELL, ***MAXWELL'S DEMON!***
YES, HE'S MINE. ***I'M SO SORRY.***
I DIDN'T MEAN FOR ANYONE TO GET HURT. I JUST WANTED TO FIT IN. MOVING IS HARD AND I THOUGHT IF I HAD SOME HELP MAKING FRIENDS, IT WOULD BE BETTER. REGARDLESS OF MY LAST NAME, MY DEMON REALLY IS A NICE GUY.
OK! I GUESS EVERYONE DESERVES A SECOND CHANCE. HI, MY NAME IS SPECTRA, YOUR FRIENDLY NEIGHBORHOOD MIDDLE SCHOOL SUPERHERO. WELCOME TO NIKOLA TESLA JR. HIGH. THINGS HERE MAY BE WEIRD, BUT AT LEAST THEY'RE NEVER BORING!
THE END

ALSO AVAILABLE FROM AT PHYSICSCENTRAL.COM

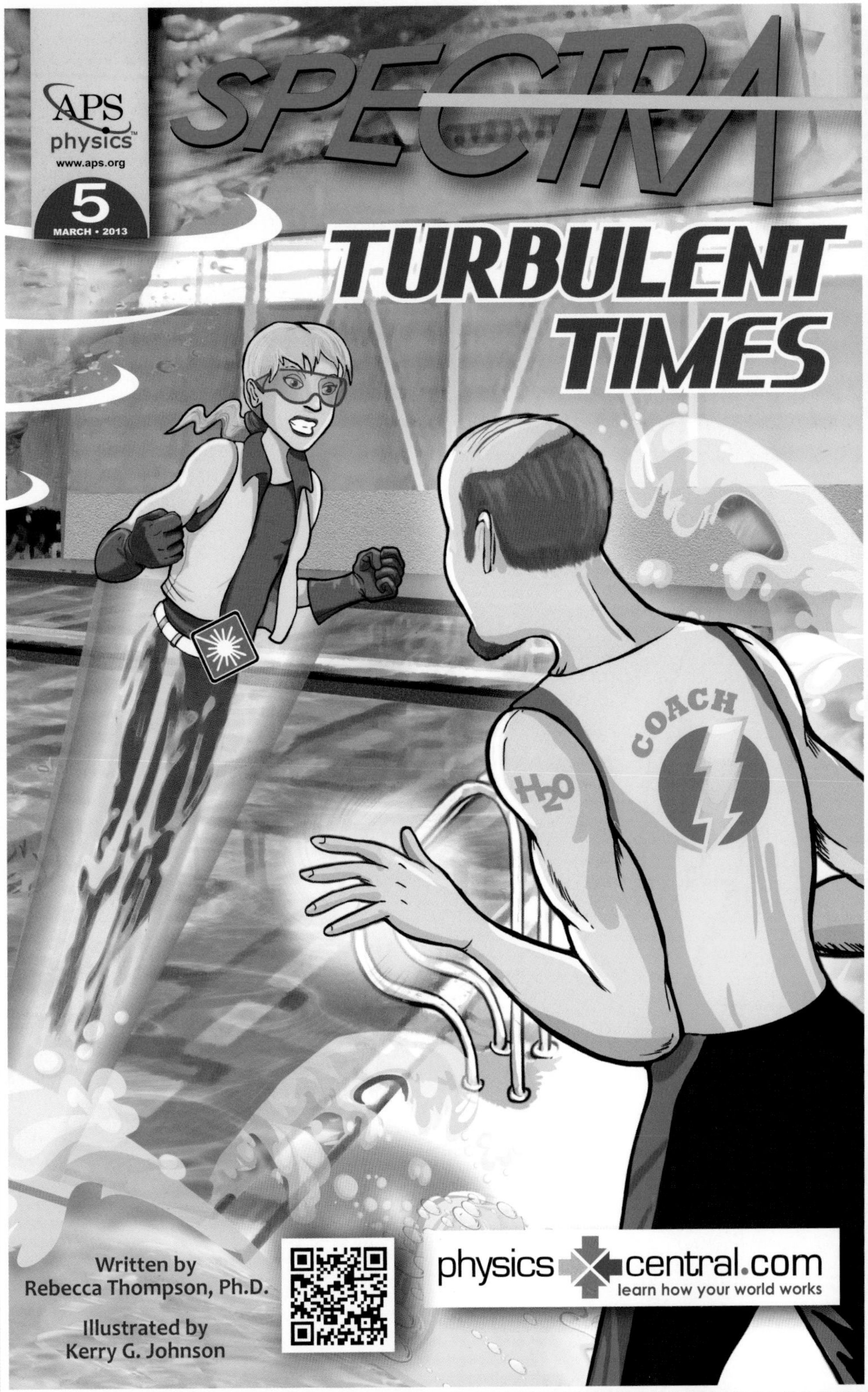
APS physics
www.aps.org
5
MARCH • 2013
SPECTRA
TURBULENT TIMES
COACH
H2O
Written by
Rebecca Thompson, Ph.D.
Illustrated by
Kerry G. Johnson
physics central.com
learn how your world works

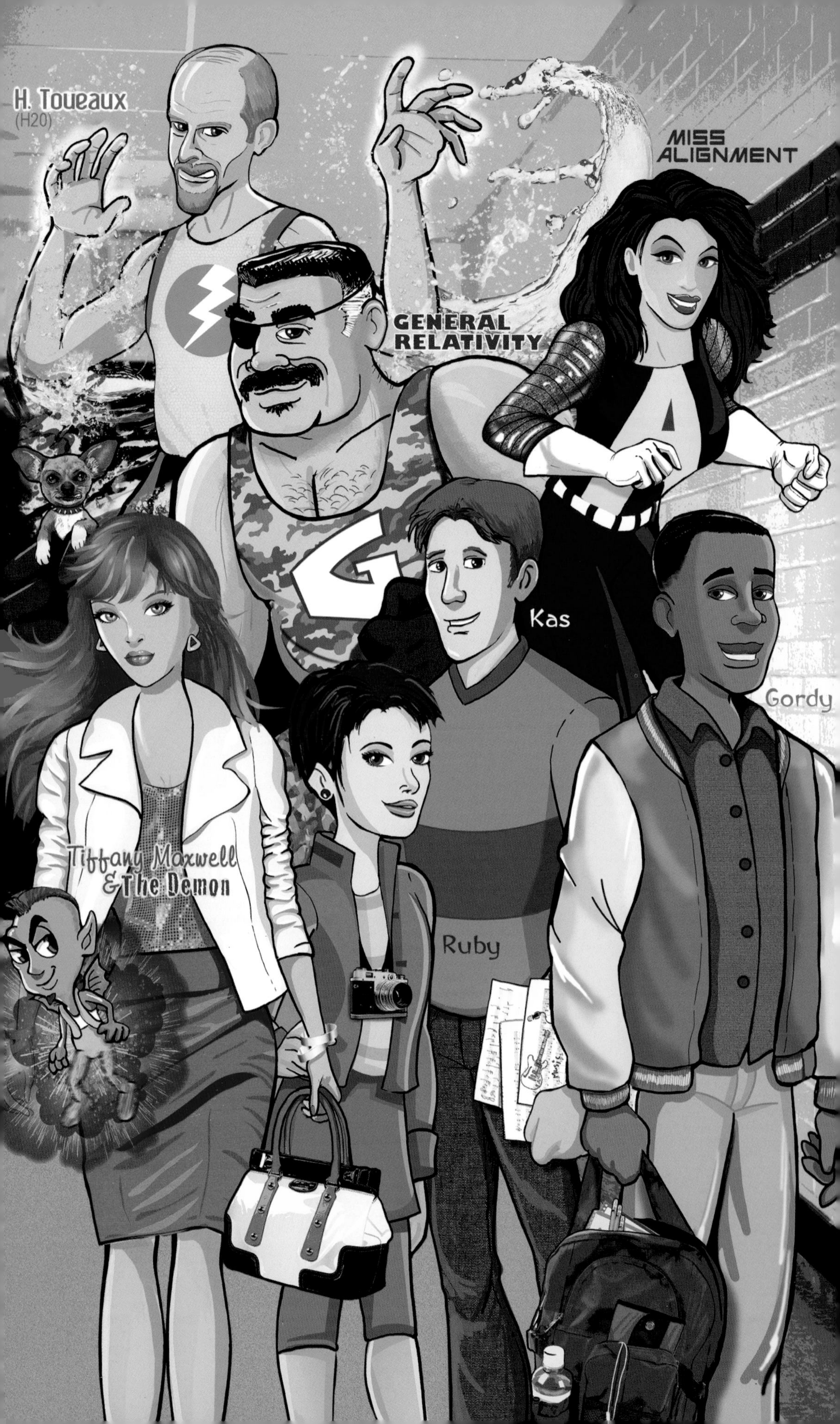
H. Toueaux
(H20)
MISS ALIGNMENT
GENERAL RELATIVITY
Kas
Gordy
Tiffany Maxwell & The Demon
Ruby